HOW TO BUILD CABINS,
LODGES, AND BUNGALOWS

HOW TO BUILD CABINS, LODGES & BUNGALOWS

COMPLETE MANUAL OF CONSTRUCTING, DECORATING, AND FURNISHING HOMES FOR RECREATION OR PROFIT

Editors of *Popular Science Monthly*

Skyhorse Publishing

spent on other forms of vacation activities. Suitable cabin sites, near streams or lakes or in the mountains, can be bought cheaply. A fraction of an acre is sufficient. If you live near a National Park, the United States Government will let you erect a cabin on a delightful spot, for a fee of a few dollars a year. Similar summer-home sites can be obtained in various state parks.

If you do not want to build a cabin or lodge for yourself, perhaps you can find profit and pleasure in erecting such structures for others. It is not every man who can find time to construct his own vacation home, so he must pay some one else to do it. That some one else may as well be you.

It is the purpose of this book to set forth a number of ideas that will be helpful to the vacation-home builder. An attempt has been made to give information of a fundamental nature. During the actual building of a cabin or similar structure, unforeseen difficulties will arise, which must be solved on the spot. That is true of any type of building, particularly where the builder is not a contractor of long experience. Although numerous floor plans and other details of design are illustrated, there is no necessity to cling doggedly to them. The creation of a cabin is a relatively simple matter, and one that permits much flexibility both in design and construction.

It is desired to express appreciation to the various government organizations, lumber associations, manufacturers and others for their invaluable assistance in providing some of the information and illustrations used in this book.

TABLE OF CONTENTS

HOW TO BUILD CABINS, LODGES, AND BUNGALOWS

HOW TO BUILD CABINS, LODGES, AND BUNGALOWS

CHAPTER I

THE CABIN MOVEMENT

THE word cabin will be used throughout this book to designate a simple structure primarily intended for recreational purposes and part-time occupancy. It will be one story high, in most cases; will consist of one, or at most three or four, rooms; seldom will have a foundation other than a few stone or concrete piers, and will be capable of being built by the amateur. A cabin will be considered as having a number of relatives, structures whose design and construction are fundamentally alike, which are neither elaborate nor expensive, and which can be built by anyone.

First and most important is the log cabin. Because the log house is so firmly rooted in American history, it will be a long time before, in the mind of the average American, any other structure can replace it as a symbol of primitive comfort. The person who conceives the idea of building a summer or vacation home invariably thinks first of a log cabin, and usually does everything within his power to obtain that type in preference to any other. Unfortunately, the scarcity of logs and cost of labor in some sections make it necessary to choose a substitute. Also, the pioneer who knows all about log-cabin building from boyhood experience cannot be found in every home or community, and the novice is hesitant about tackling anything that looks as formidable as building a house of logs.

In reality, the erection of a log cabin is not difficult, and need not be costly. When it is properly put up,

Substantial cottage, showing the best manner of making corner joints. Casement window opens out flat against the wall

the builder has something that will last for years, perhaps for generations. Considerable space is given in this book to log cabins. This is primarily because the log structure can be used as a basis for so many other types. For instance, there is on the market a log siding or weatherboarding that permits the construction of faithful imitations of log houses. So if real logs are not available, the vacation cabin can be a wooden framework covered with this type of material, without losing much of the charm of a real log house.

Log siding, usually made of pine or redwood, consists of interlocking boards so milled that their outer surfaces are curved, like sections ripped from real logs. Such boards lend themselves to a wide variety of uses. They can be employed outside to simulate logs laid horizontally or vertically, and on the inside for creating distinctive wall surfaces. Log siding can be stained, painted, varnished, or left to weather naturally. It will not decay, either because of inherent properties or because of treatment given it during manufacture. A modernized log cabin consists of a framework of 2 by 4's and similar sawn timbers, covered outside and perhaps inside with log siding. This siding is made in various widths, so that it can be applied in random fashion to give still more realistic imitations of log walls.

Another type of log cabin of interest to the modern owner is the pre-cut variety. Real logs, usually cedar because of that wood's resistance to decay and insect attack, are employed. The corner notches and other constructional details are cut at a mill. The logs arrive at the cabin site ready to erect without laborious chopping and sawing. Some companies provide expert supervision or labor when the customer desires it, and deliver the cabin complete, even to furniture.

Hunting and fishing lodges may be of logs or of simple frame construction, with an outer wall covering of almost anything from log siding to plain boards set

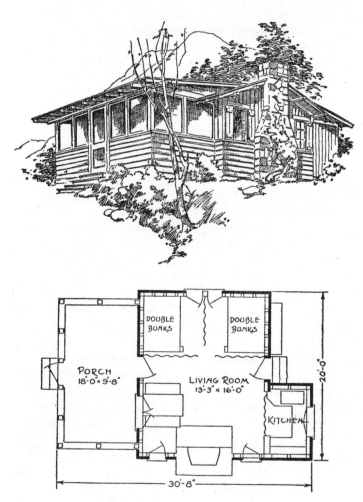

Simple cabin with kitchenette. This makes an especially attractive summer home. The floor plan shows the disposition of inside space (*Courtesy, Shevlin Pine Sales Co.*)

horizontally or vertically. Such lodges frequently consist of a single room, with cooking and bunking facilities arranged to make the most of the space available. Sometimes a type of construction is used that permits the lodge to be torn down and moved to another location. This is a valuable feature because a good hunting or fishing locality may not always remain that way. A hunting or fishing lodge does not differ fundamentally from a simple cabin, tourist home, or summer cottage, so that designs for these structures may be used interchangeably.

Bungalows and summer cottages may be of logs, but more frequently are frame structures with outer wall surfaces covered with log siding, plain siding, shingles, or plain boards arranged in a pleasing manner. They can even be of stone, when such construction is economically possible. Rammed earth is another cheap but little-used type of wall construction that might be employed.

Because the motorist of today demands something better than a tent and cheaper than a conventional hotel, tourist cabins have become a familiar sight along our highways. A really attractive tourist home can be built for $200 or so, and will pay for itself in one season if it is built at a strategic point. The same fundamental designs employed for vacation homes can be utilized for tourist purposes, with some alterations in interior arrangement.

Wayside stands, where farm products and refreshments are sold to motorists, are offshoots of the genuine cabin. Their construction is not essentially different. Provide any simple cabin with an open front, a counter, and perhaps a projecting roof, and you have a

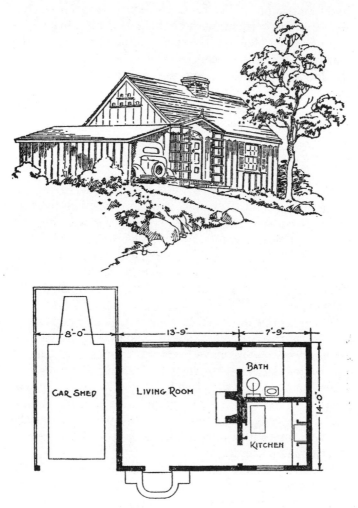

Cottage built of sawed lumber. It makes a desirable hunting **lodge** or vacation cabin. Its simplicity is evident in the floor plan
(*Courtesy, Shevlin Pine Sales Co.*)

CHAPTER II

WHERE AND WHEREWITH TO BUILD

UNFAVORABLY located, the finest cabin in the world will be a disappointment. Selecting a site is a matter of great importance. For summer-home use, some of the factors affecting the location include accessibility, drainage, water supply, cooling breezes, wooded areas, lakes, streams, and vistas or scenery. Some thought may be given also to the safety factor: the nearness of dangerous cliffs, avenues of escape in event of a forest fire, flood menace, and protection from storms.

Although it is desirable to have a vacation retreat far from any road, you must consider the matter of accessibility. In the first place, materials used in construction must be hauled to the site. Later, guests and supplies must be transported to the cabin, usually in automobiles. Keep in mind the fact that roads and trails that are excellent in dry weather may become impassable when it rains, or during winter months when the ground is not frozen.

It is a frequent practice to place a cabin on a hillside, where it nestles snugly against the earth, protected from storms by trees and elevated ground. Unless care is exercised, the cabin owner may awake some stormy night with the impression that he is on a houseboat. Sites in the direct path of wet-weather streams

and drainage ditches should be avoided. To take care
of normal drainage, grade the area around the cabin
so that water runs away from it. Between the cabin
and area from which water is likely to flow, create a
water barrier. This can be a shallow ditch, a masonry
wall, or a basin formed by filling in around the cabin.
Water should be able to escape from the barrier by
flowing around the cabin yard.

In preparing the logs for your cabin, two men with a crosscut saw
can do the work easily and rapidly

To assure health protection, make certain that the
water supply is adequate and safe. It seldom is safe to
use water from streams. Springs are satisfactory if
there is no seepage of waste matter into them from
above. A dug or drilled well is perhaps the best form
of water supply. But whatever the source, it will pay
you to have the water tested once or twice a year.
In most states, this will be done by the county or state

health department without charge. You simply procure a sterilized bottle from the local health officer, fill it with the water, and mail it to the place designated.

The location of porches and other matters of orientation will be determined largely by the direction from which cooling breezes blow, points from which the most

Logs can be dressed to any shape desired by using a sharp ax as indicated in the illustration

beautiful scenery can be enjoyed, position of shore of lakes and streams, and the presence of large trees or other natural formations.

From the standpoint of safety, it would be unwise to build a cabin on the brink of a cliff, or at a point where a dangerous rock formation or steep slope must be negotiated to reach the site. Do not place the building under a leaning tree that might fall, unless the tree can be removed. Avoid, likewise, overhanging rocks and earthen banks. Make inquiry about the height of flood waters from near-by streams and note whether the site is in a pocket that might become a lake if the rainfall is heavy. In mountainous country, the danger of snow slides and landslides must be taken into consideration.

Another important factor is sanitation. Outside toilets should be placed in a secluded spot not too close to the cabin, and should be below the level of springs, and at least 100 feet away from all sources of drinking water. Do not place the toilet near the main roadway or approach to the cabin. These suggestions apply to chemical toilets, pit toilets, septic tanks, and garbage pits.

When erecting a cabin, keep in mind the fact that you may want to enlarge it later. Because of its informal and rustic nature, the average cabin can ramble all over the place and still look attractive. It is better, however, to follow some definite plan, and to leave space for possible later additions.

Preserve, as far as possible, the natural appearance of surroundings. Let all trees stand, except the dead ones, and refrain from trimming off limbs that are close to the ground. Clear away only the underbrush and shrubbery where absolutely necessary. Usually the landscaping can be improved by transplanting shrubbery, so as to create natural screens separating the cabin from the roadway or from other cabins, to conceal outbuildings, and effect other improvements. When fences are built, they should be of rough poles, to preserve the rustic appearance of the surroundings. The same applies to outdoor furniture, boat docks, etc.

The matter of tools is not a difficult one to solve, when it comes to the actual erection of a cabin. A log house, being primitive in nature, can be built with the aid of only an ax and a crosscut saw. However, some elaboration on these fundamental tools is desirable. An adz may be helpful. Old-time cabin builders used

This is a bad location for a cabin as the hillside drains water into the site. Also, the bottom logs are in contact with the ground

a broad-ax for hewing logs flat. This consisted of a wide-bladed ax head fitted with a hickory handle steamed and bent slightly outward, so that it would not be struck against the log and be broken. When these handles got wet, they often straightened out again. If you cannot procure a broad-ax, either a broad hatchet with 5- or 6-in. blade, or an ordinary ax can be used for hewing. A wide blade is necessary in order to produce a smooth surface.

A shingle-splitting tool was employed a great deal in earlier times, but you probably will buy your shingles or other roofing material. For cutting logs, a two-man crosscut saw is desirable. You will find it wearisome to work logs with a hand-saw although such a tool is useful when handling small poles, framing

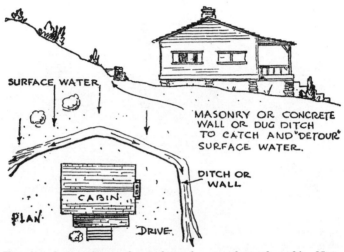

Here is a better site as the drainage is away from the cabin. Note the building is set on concrete supports and a restraining wall diverts the water from the hill

windows and doors, etc. A heavy hammer, for driving spikes, is necessary. Some forms of construction require that the logs be nailed together at intervals, the spikes being driven through holes bored part way through them. For this purpose an auger and a bar or rod of iron a foot long and about $5/8$ in. in greatest diameter are used. A sufficiently strong block and tackle can be used to raise logs into place on the wall.

The upper pulley can be mounted on a tripod made of poles, or attached to the part of the wall already in place. With this useful device, two men can put up a cabin that, without it, would require a half-dozen or more men, working with forked or pointed poles. A small trowel for chinking cracks between logs is desirable.

For building other types of cabins from mill-sawed lumber, the usual assortment of carpenters' tools is required. These include hammer, rip and crosscut hand saw, hatchet, steel tape, steel square, plumb line and bob, level, chisels, plane, and so on. Sectional or ready-cut cabins, which can be purchased from some dealers, require to erect them little more than a hammer, and perhaps a wrench for tightening nuts on bolts.

If you go into the business of building vacation cabins and lodges, you will find a power saw, with perhaps a jointer unit attached, a great convenience, and at least as serviceable as an extra helper. An 8-in. circular saw on a suitable stand does not cost a great deal. With it you can rip, crosscut, dado and otherwise process stock in excess of 2 in. thick. A saw of this type together with a 4-in. jointer, mounted on a rugged steel stand, can be purchased for less than $70. For about $40, you can get a 7/10-horsepower, four-cycle gasoline engine that will operate the saw, and any other power machinery you may want to use. The saw-jointer unit and engine can be hauled to the job in a small truck.

CHAPTER III

FOUNDATIONS

LIKE the chain that had a weak link, more than one log cabin or summer bungalow has had its life shortened by a poor foundation, or no foundation at all. Builders of log cabins sometimes lay the sill logs directly on the ground. Now it happens that one of the easiest ways to make wood decay is to leave it in contact with the earth. Moisture, collecting between the wood and ground, creates conditions ideal for the growth of decay-producing fungi. Hence a log cabin, built flat on the ground, will, in a few years, start to fall apart. The same applies to any other kind of structure. In addition to decay, there are certain insects, such as termites, that delight in finding a building with no foundation.

A common form of support for cabins consists of piers made of two or more flat stones laid one on the other. A single stone is not much better than no stone at all, because moisture can still reach the wood and cause decay to set in. When two stones are used, the joint between them stops the rise of moisture and the top stone will remain dry. Do not cement the stones together.

Another support that has been used but is not generally recommended by building experts is a post of cedar or other wood. Some woods, such as cedar, locust, redwood, and pine, have sufficient natural resistance to decay and insect attack to permit their being used without particular protection. Other woods should be creosoted, and it is not a bad idea to use creosote on the woods that are naturally resistant.

The creosote can be applied with a long-handled paint brush bound with wire, or a small, soft-bristled broom. Heat the creosote in a large pail or kettle until it is very hot but not boiling (about 200 degrees Fahrenheit). Do not let it boil over and become ignited. An open fire, with the creosote container supported on a grate or hung from a crane, can be used, if reasonable care is exercised. Apply two coats of the preservative, letting the first one dry well before the second is applied. Flow the creosote over the wood, and work it into every crack and hole. After the wood is treated, handle it carefully so as not to break the protective layer. This method of applying creosote can be used for other parts of a building. Coal-tar creosote, a heavy, brownish-black oil, is the type to use.

Posts used as piers should be about a foot in diameter, and long enough to extend a yard or so into the ground. At the bottom of the hole dug for such a pier, place a flat stone, to form a footing. This stone should be somewhat larger than the post.

Perhaps the best pier is made of reinforced concrete or of stone-and-cement masonry. The pier should extend below the frost line, or preferably down to solid rock or dense gravel. This is particularly true of a support for a heavy log cabin.

For a concrete pier not resting on rock, first dig a hole about 24 in. square, and deep enough to extend below the frost line. If the house is to rest but a few inches above the ground, build forms of 1-in. lumber

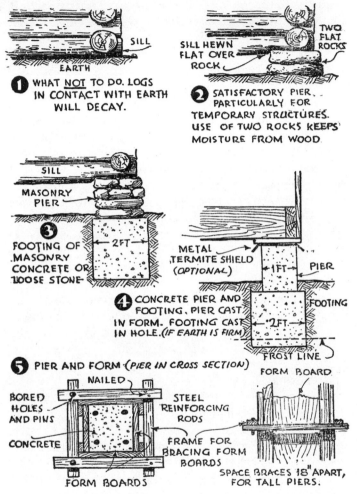

1 WHAT <u>NOT</u> TO DO. LOGS IN CONTACT WITH EARTH WILL DECAY.

SILL

EARTH

2 SATISFACTORY PIER. PARTICULARLY FOR TEMPORARY STRUCTURES. USE OF TWO ROCKS KEEPS MOISTURE FROM WOOD.

SILL HEWN FLAT OVER ROCK

TWO FLAT ROCKS

3 FOOTING OF MASONRY CONCRETE OR LOOSE STONE

SILL

MASONRY PIER

2 FT

4 CONCRETE PIER AND FOOTING. PIER CAST IN FORM. FOOTING CAST IN HOLE. (IF EARTH IS FIRM)

METAL TERMITE SHIELD (OPTIONAL)

1 FT

PIER

FOOTING

2 FT

FROST LINE

5 PIER AND FORM (PIER IN CROSS SECTION)

NAILED

BORED HOLES AND PINS

CONCRETE

STEEL REINFORCING RODS

FRAME FOR BRACING FORM BOARDS

FORM BOARDS

FORM BOARD

SPACE BRACES 18" APART, FOR TALL PIERS.

These various illustrations show, first, how not to lay the bottom logs of your cabin, and then the proper methods that will insure long life to a cabin's foundation

that reach to the bottom of the hole and extend for the required distance above the ground. Another way, which saves form lumber, is to extend the boards just far enough below the ground surface to prevent the concrete from escaping beneath them. Use a 1:2:4 mixture of concrete to fill the form. That is, mix 1 part by volume of Portland cement, 2 parts coarse, clean sand, and 4 parts gravel or broken stone. Add water until the concrete will just flow—until it is about the consistency of mush. It is not a bad idea to reinforce the piers by inserting four ¾-in. steel bars, arranging them near the corners and tying them in position with heavy iron wire.

If the pier is to extend for a considerable distance above the ground, as it will on the lower side of a sloping site, the following method of pier construction can be employed: First make a footing by digging a 2-ft. square hole below the frost line and filling it with concrete to within 6 inches of the surface of the ground, using the mixture given. Then, with flat boards, build a form for a post 1 ft. square, extending from the base to the desired height. Brace it with outside frames every 18 in. Insert four reinforcing rods, placing them 2 in. or so inside the corners, and tying them together at 12-in. intervals with heavy wire or ¼-in. rods. You can fasten these rods to the larger ones with baling wire or similar small wire. Extend cross rods at intervals until their ends touch the form so that the reinforcing network will be held away from the wood. Fill the form with the 1:2:4 concrete mixture, tamping it in place with a paddle, and manipulating it so that the large pebbles or rock pieces do

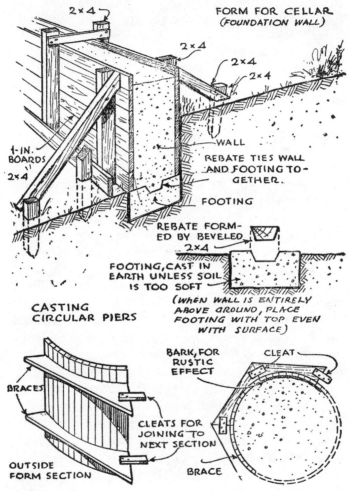

2×4

FORM FOR CELLAR
(FOUNDATION WALL)

2×4

2×4
2×4

4-IN.
BOARDS

2×4

WALL

REBATE TIES WALL
AND FOOTING TO-
GETHER.

FOOTING

REBATE FORM-
ED BY BEVELED
2×4

FOOTING, CAST IN
EARTH UNLESS SOIL
IS TOO SOFT

(WHEN WALL IS ENTIRELY
ABOVE GROUND, PLACE
FOOTING WITH TOP EVEN
WITH SURFACE)

CASTING
CIRCULAR PIERS

BARK, FOR
RUSTIC
EFFECT

CLEAT

BRACES

CLEATS FOR
JOINING TO
NEXT SECTION

OUTSIDE
FORM SECTION

BRACE

Since a cellar is desirable, the illustration at top shows how the
foundation wall for a cellar is built. Drawing above shows manner of
casting circular piers for use in foundations

not remain near the surface. Let the pier set for several days before starting the cabin structure.

When it is desired to preserve the rustic atmosphere demanded by some types of cabins, particularly log ones, the discordant note introduced by square, plain concrete piers can be eliminated by some form of camouflage. Shrubs can be planted where they will hide the piers from view, or vines can be placed so that they will grow over the concrete. Virginia Creeper (five-leafed ivy) is excellent. For a log house, the piers can be made round, and the concrete painted or otherwise colored to harmonize with the logs. For instance, a chocolate brown, that ought not to produce a discordant note with rustic construction, can be made by mixing burnt umber with the concrete in about the proportion of 4 lbs. of umber to every 100 pounds of cement. The ingenious craftsman can make artificial concrete logs by lining cylindrical forms with rough bark placed with the rough side next to the pier material. Probably the bark will have to be torn from the pier by force, because some parts of it will be imbedded in such a manner that it will not loosen easily. Still another expedient is to apply strips of bark to the exposed surfaces of ordinary piers, fastening the pieces by wires running behind, or by some other feasible means.

If you prefer a stone pier, first make a concrete footing as described or else a loose stone footing. This latter type is made by digging a hole about 2 ft. square to a depth of about 3 ft., and filling it with pieces of stone carefully arranged and compacted so that they will not compress when weight is applied. A loose-stone footing can be used beneath concrete piers or flat stones.

After the footing is in place, lay up the stones with cement mortar. Whole or split field stones, those gathered from beaches, or quarried sandstone can be used. The mortar is made by mixing Portland cement and sand in about the proportion of 1 part cement to 3 or 4 parts sand. The addition of a little lime putty will make the mortar easier to work. A suitable mixture consists of 6 parts cement, 24 parts sand and ½ to 1 part lime putty. Ordinary lime mortar consists of about 1 part lime and 4 parts sand with sufficient water to make a paste. Do not use lime mortar for chimney and fireplace construction. Whatever the mortar you employ, mix the ingredients thoroughly. To do less is a waste of time and material, and a possible source of danger as well. Wet the stones before applying mortar.

Spacing of piers should be in proportion to the load carried. For log cabins, the supports should be placed at every corner and at intervals of 6 ft. or so along the walls. Lower parts of the sill logs are hewn flat at the points where they rest on the piers.

Where a more elaborate cabin is desired, and the added cost is not prohibitive, solid concrete or masonry walls can be used instead of piers. If masonry is used, make sure that the walls are sufficiently massive, that mortar joints between stones do not form continuous lines that might crack open, and that solid stones or bonds extend all the way through the wall at intervals, say one stone for every 8 sq. ft. of wall surface.

Concrete walls for log cabins, according to recommendations of the U. S. Department of Agriculture, should be 2 or 3 in. thicker than the width of logs

used for the sills and walls, and in no case less than
8 in. thick. Width of the footing or bottom of the
foundation will depend to some extent on the nature
of the soil, but generally should be 8 in. wider than
the wall thickness. If the soil is very soft, a wider
footing may be necessary, or piers may be extended
down at intervals to bedrock or denser soil or gravel
strata. Inspection of other buildings in the vicinity
will reveal much about the type of construction demanded by conditions.

Whatever the type of foundation, it is essential that
proper ventilation be provided beneath the floor, to
prevent decay of sills, joists, and other wood parts.
Some cabin owners block the spaces between piers
with masonry, lattice work, shingled panels or other
construction, to improve appearance. This is permis-
sible provided ventilating openings are left. These can
be screened holes about the size of the largest face of
a common brick (4 by 8 in.) spaced a few feet apart,
the screens serving to exclude insects and small animals. When a cellar is built, the walls can be solid
except for the normal window and door openings.

Termites or "white ants" are attacking wood buildings in many localities. One way of protecting against
them is by proper foundation construction and separation of the wood portion of the building from the
foundation by sheet metal. Details of termite protection, as well as protection against other insect pests,
are given in a later chapter.

CHAPTER IV

LOG CABIN MATERIALS

WHEN building a log cabin, the first thing to do is to get the logs. This may not be as easy as it sounds in some localities, particularly in regions far removed from extensive forests. Local lumber dealers, telephone, telegraph and power companies, and owners of farms and wooded lots within reasonable hauling distance, are among the sources of logs when they must be purchased. If the cabin is to be built in the woods where standing timber is available, carefully inspect all available trees to determine whether their sales value is greater than their value as sources of cabin logs. For instance, you would not want to cut down a walnut tree just to get wood for cabin walls, because walnut lumber is worth 75 cents or so a board foot. If you are erecting a cabin in a national or state forest, it is necessary to get the approval of local forest authorities before you can cut trees for logs.

Among the logs suitable for cabin construction are cedar, tamarack, balsam, hemlock, and pine. These woods are easily worked and not too heavy. Hickory, oak, and various other hardwoods are just as durable, but their weight and hardness makes them undesirable. Among the woods not suitable for cabin construction because they are not long-lived are birch, aspen, willow, cottonwood, and basswood.

34

Select logs that are straight and have only a slight taper from base to top. It would be ideal if logs with no taper at all were available in quantity, but this is unlikely. Logs with considerable taper can be used if no other kind is procurable. They will require somewhat more chinking. If you want to spend the time and effort required to build a hewn-log cabin, extreme tapering is not a serious matter because the log can be made uniform in thickness by cutting more wood from the base end.

Logs and poles from 4 to 12 in. in diameter are suitable for cabin construction. The larger ones usually are used in walls, while the smaller sizes go into roofs in the form of rafters, and in other parts where massiveness is not desirable or essential. Logs from 1 to 4 ft. longer than the walls in which they are to be used are necessary when corner construction calls for projecting ends. There are some types of construction requiring logs of the same length as the walls. Avoid excessively long walls that require logs too heavy to be handled conveniently. About 20 ft. is a desirable limit, and it seldom is necessary to make a cabin room larger than that. Although lap joints or other means can be used for fastening short lengths of logs together to produce long walls, this should be avoided because it weakens the walls.

The proper time to cut logs, and the subsequent treatment to be given them to prevent decay and insect damage, are determined by the way in which they are to be finished. The bark can be left on to preserve the rustic appearance; or it can be peeled off and the logs left bare or hewed to produce flat surfaces.

Logs that are to retain their bark should be cut in

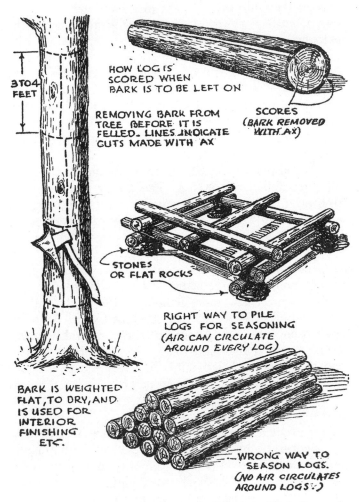

3 TO 4 FEET

HOW LOG IS SCORED WHEN BARK IS TO BE LEFT ON

REMOVING BARK FROM TREE BEFORE IT IS FELLED. LINES INDICATE CUTS MADE WITH AX

SCORES (BARK REMOVED WITH AX)

STONES OR FLAT ROCKS

RIGHT WAY TO PILE LOGS FOR SEASONING (AIR CAN CIRCULATE AROUND EVERY LOG)

BARK IS WEIGHTED FLAT, TO DRY, AND IS USED FOR INTERIOR FINISHING ETC.

WRONG WAY TO SEASON LOGS. (NO AIR CIRCULATES AROUND LOGS)

Manner of removing bark from tree before it is felled, the scoring of logs, and the right way of piling them to dry are shown above

the fall, about the time of the first frost, according to government forestry experts. During October and November is a satisfactory time in most localities. If cut in late summer, the bark will remain on, but the logs are likely to become infested with destructive insects.

Difficulty sometimes arises as a result of the bark peeling off. One way of checking this is to score the logs. This is done by removing a narrow strip of bark from two opposite sides, for the entire length. Then pile the logs in the shade, in such manner that air will circulate freely through them, and let them season until the next spring or summer. When the logs are used for walls, the scored strips can be placed at top and bottom, where they will be concealed by the chinking. A few days after cutting, and again a short time before the logs are used, paint all ends, knots and scored areas with coal-tar creosote, to preserve the wood. When the bark develops a tendency to peel off, or when the logs are not scored, tack the bark in place with large-head roofing nails, spacing them about a foot apart each way.

Trees whose trunks are to be used as peeled logs should be cut in the winter, when the sap is down. If cut in the spring, the wood will be attacked by organisms that cause decay and stain. Aside from the less rustic appearance, peeled logs are better than unpeeled ones. One reason is that they are less likely to be attacked by insects. Trees felled during certain seasons may become infested with beetles. The insects drill holes in the bark and lay their eggs in them. Such invasions are indicated by the presence of the holes and of wood particles resembling sawdust, which fall out of the logs. The eggs hatch into larvae that feed on the inner bark, boring tunnels in every direction. This causes the outer bark to loosen and fall off. More than that, the grubs often bore into the heartwood and sapwood of the logs, destroying them before the wood is completely seasoned, usually a matter of a few months. Methods of combating such pests are discussed in another chapter.

Peeled or hewn logs are finished in a variety of ways. Sometimes they are left to weather naturally. It is, however, better to employ some preservative that will act to prevent decay and insect attack, although peeled logs are less likely to be damaged by insects and decay organisms than those with the bark left on. Preservatives should be applied during construction, when all parts can be reached. Later applications, after the building has been completed, can be made with greater ease when the logs are peeled. Paint, stain, and creosote are among the materials used for preserving logs. Paint is not desirable because it destroys the desired rustic appearance. Creosote is effective, but its odor is persistent and not pleasant, making it undesirable for dwellings. Stain is perhaps the best because it acts as a preservative, can be of a color that produces the effect of naturally weathered wood, and does not give off a persistent odor. Whether or not the logs are peeled,—and particularly if they are not, the cuts made in forming corner joints should be treated with a preservative. Paint can be used when it will not show.

When the logs are left exposed on interior wall surfaces, they absorb much light, causing the gloomy appearance that is characteristic of most log cabins. This can be eliminated somewhat by applying varnish or shellac to the bark or peeled surfaces. The smooth coating reflects light better than the untreated surfaces. Do not stain peeled logs dark on interior walls. If a stain is used at all it should be extremely light in tone. Application of varnish alone will produce on most woods a color that is mellow enough to please everyone. Chinking materials should be light in color where they show on interior surfaces.

If your cabin has been in use for some time, and the bark starts to fall off because of improper earlier treatment, nail it back in place. It is not a bad idea to treat the back of the bark pieces, and the surface of the wood with creosote or some other preservative before doing this.

Available logs and poles do not always permit the widest choice of materials. You may have to be satisfied with short logs or with logs so crooked that they have to be cut into short lengths before they can be used. Large diameters may be lacking. The taper may be excessive.

When such conditions exist, they often can be counteracted by proper design. Although it is easier to lay up a cabin wall with long logs and then cut out the windows and doors, it is possible to employ short lengths, using them about the door and window frames as the work progresses. By employing a design that calls for a great many windows, short material can be utilized for intervening panels, making long logs necessary only for sills and for use above the openings. A log house should be low and rambling for best appearance, so that much material is not required above door height. Old-time cabins, and a great many of more recent construction, have windows that are too small and too few. This detracts from the outside appearance and makes the interior gloomy. Install all the windows you can without destroying large wall spaces necessary for beds, etc., and make them of a shape and size that will admit plenty of light and still harmonize with the general appearance. You will need fewer logs if you do, and the logs probably will be the major item of cost. Casement windows opening outward are better for log cabins than other types.

In addition to walls with logs laid horizontally, a type of construction frequently employed makes use of logs running vertically, their lower ends resting on the sills and their upper ends supporting the roof plate. This type of construction can be employed when short lengths are to be worked in.

In addition to the materials for the walls and foundations, you will need some of the following, the exact requirements depending on the type of construction and the extent to which available poles, logs, and slabs are employed: 2- by 4-in. boards for miscellaneous uses; 2- by 6-in. to 2- by 12-in. timbers for joists and roof-ridge pieces; some 1-in. lumber ranging in width from 6 in. to 12 in., for roof sheathing and various other uses; some 2-in. lumber for false door jambs and window frames, the width depending on the thickness of logs; tongue-and-groove ceiling, for covering interior wall surfaces and making partitions; tongue-and-groove flooring of 4-in. size, or in random widths, for floors. Nails in assorted sizes, including some large spikes of about 40-penny size; doors, window sashes, and door and window hardware; some kind of roof covering, ranging from split shingles to composition roofing; painted sheet metal for use under roof covering at ridges and valleys, and for flashing around chimneys or stove pipes. Doubtless there are other items for which a need will develop as the building progresses. You may find it difficult to estimate, beforehand, the exact quantity and kind of materials needed. This is true of most buildings, and particularly so of the cabin that is not being erected in strict accordance with a specific plan, but is being permitted to grow more or less naturally, like the trees from which it is made.

CHAPTER V

LOG CABIN WALLS

L OG-CABIN walls are of two general types. In one
   the logs stand on end and in the other they lie
horizontally. Cabins with logs vertically sometimes are
called pole houses, probably because small logs or
poles are more conveniently used in this manner than
in a horizontal position. Among the advantages of the
pole-house construction is the greater ease of erecting
the walls, and the fact that short logs can be utilized.
The forming of window and door openings is merely a
matter of omitting logs. The biggest arguments against
the pole house are its relative weakness and the fact
that it is somewhat more difficult to chink than the
conventional type.

Because cabin walls with logs placed vertically are
pleasing in appearance and can be treated architectur-
ally in a considerable variety of ways, and because of
the other favorable points, the summer home, hunting
lodge or lake bungalow might very well be a pole
house. The objection that the construction is inherently weak can be overcome by careful spiking of the
various elements as they are placed. As for the chinking, a little attention to fitting the logs will make most
of that easy.

After you have completed the foundation walls or
piers, and made certain that they are level all the way
around, the next job, and the first operation in wall-

building, is to construct the sills. These are logs laid on the foundation to form the bases for the walls. Sometimes true sills extend only beneath two opposite walls; sometimes all around—as in a pole house. With a broadax or an ordinary ax having a long cutting edge, hew each of the sill logs flat on top and bottom. Make the top as smooth as possible, for on it must rest the squarely sawed ends of the vertical logs. In

An example of a cabin built with upright logs. In this case it would be better had the rear of the cabin been raised clear of the ground

hewing, the amount of wood necessary to be removed will depend on the straightness of the log and the amount of taper. Use the soundest, straightest, and least tapering logs for sills. Frequently it is desirable to hew the log on four sides to produce a square timber whose width is about the same as that of the vertical poles, or slightly greater. At the corners, where the sill pieces come together, make a lap joint by cutting wood from each piece to a depth of half the thickness of the pieces, and for a distance from the end of each piece equal to the width of the other piece. Fasten the joint with heavy spikes, or by boring holes and inserting heavy wood or steel pins. It is not a bad idea to apply creosote paint or other preservative to the wood surfaces at the joints.

A plate is a log laid horizontally, resting on the upper ends of the vertical logs of a wall. It is constructed exactly like the sill. After the sill is finished,

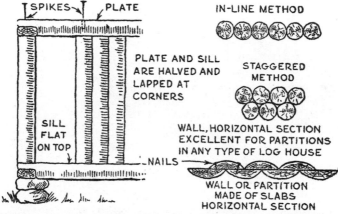

Here is the best manner of setting logs in an upright position in a cabin wall. Manner of making inside partitions is also shown

set a vertical log at each corner, fastening it to the sill with heavy spikes (something like 40-penny size) driven at an angle through the post and into the sill. This is called toe-nailing. Temporary braces can be used to give rigidity and safety during subsequent operations. These braces can be 1- by 6-in. boards set at an angle of 45 degrees to the sill and corner post. Hoist the plate logs or timbers to the tops of the corner posts and spike them in place. Incidentally, the plates and sills can be constructed of 2-in. planks nailed together until the desired thickness is produced, if suitable logs are not available. It is highly important that the plates and sills be level. See that they are, before you proceed with the placing of vertical pieces.

The poles or logs should be no less than 4 in. in diameter. It is desirable that their tapers be uniform, as this makes construction easier. For a good, weather-proof job, hew each log on opposite sides, and fit it carefully against the neighboring one. Cut each log so that it will fit snugly between sill and plate, and fasten it in position by driving spikes diagonally into the sill. These can be driven so that the next pole will cover them. Ends of the poles should be treated to prevent rotting. Creosote applied as described is excellent, or paint can be used.

When a point is reached' where a door or window is to be made, hew the last pole so that the side next to the door frame is plumb. Determine when this condition is obtained by testing the pole with a carpenter's level. Allow sufficient space for the door or window casing, and begin the next series of poles. Continue this until the walls are finished. Remaining details of construction are practically the same as for the horizontal type of log cabin.

If the construction of a log house were complicated, the early settlers, with their few simple tools, would have developed some other type of dwelling. The chief ingredient is heavy work. Getting the logs into position can be accomplished without difficulty by two men using a block and tackle. For the average cabin, the wall-building should not require more than a week or two of time.

Log-cabin walls rest on sills and are topped by plates. In some forms of construction there are true sills and plates along only two opposite walls, nearly always the longer ones. The bottom logs across the ends may be somewhat above the level of the sill logs along the sides, and therefore elevated a few inches above the foundation. This is determined by the type of joint employed. It is, however, a good idea to halve the ends of the bottom logs and make lap joints at corners, to produce a sill all around. When a hip roof

How to cut in a casement window that will swing out is shown in this illustration

is used, it rests on plates extending along all four sides; when a simple gable roof is used, it rests mainly on plates running along the two longer sides. Hew the top of each sill flat and level. Set the sill logs carefully on the piers or foundation walls, and make sure that they do not rock. This is accomplished by proper hewing of the under side of the log at the points of contact with the foundations.

The ways in which logs may be locked together at the corners are numerous, as indicated by the drawings. Of all the designs shown, No. 6 is probably the best because it is simple in design and therefore can be cut easily with an ax, and because it does not catch and hold water. This matter of retaining water is important, for it may mean the difference between long and short cabin life. The No. 6 joint was a favorite with old-time cabin builders. It can be cut with the aid of a saw by the modern builder who is not particularly skilful with an ax.

The joint shown in No. 4 is not completely interlocking, but has the advantage of not retaining water. Spikes have to be driven into the joints, to make them absolutely rigid. In No. 7 is shown a method of using logs so that end and side courses are even, and not staggered as with most other types. No. 1 is a simple corner construction in which the logs are cut square and held together by vertical timbers spiked to their ends. A small log or quarter section of a larger one is used to fill the angle and produce a finished appearance. This joint, as well as that in No. 7, lacks strength because it is difficult if not impossible to lock it securely with spikes. Therefore, it is necessary to fasten the logs together by driving spikes at intervals along their lengths. First a ¾-in. hole is bored halfway through the top log, and a large spike inserted into it and driven through the remainder of the bored log and into the next one, with the aid of a ⅝-in. steel bar and heavy hammer. Joint No. 8 is a simple one and reasonably strong if care is taken in spiking. In appearance it is not quite comparable with some of the other joints that permit the full end of each log to show.

The extent of projection of the logs at the corners will be determined both by the type of notching and the personal taste of the builder. Usually the logs should be cut from 1 to 2 ft. longer than the walls, permitting a projection at each corner of 6 to 12 in. Measurements are made from outside surfaces of the intersecting walls. By letting the bottom logs project more than the top ones, and graduating those in between so that a uniform slope is produced in a line

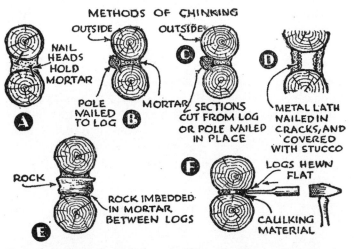

Various methods of chinking and calking the logs in the cabin are shown. Any method will serve if it is carefully done

connecting the ends, an unusual effect is obtained, and an impression of great solidity is produced.

When plenty of logs are available, it is customary to cut window and door openings after the walls are laid. Logs are placed so that bad spots will be cut out, when possible. The top log of the opening is either cut away for the full width of the opening, or deeply notched at each extremity of the opening, so that a saw blade can be passed through. A 2- by 6-in. plank is nailed temporarily to the logs in such manner that the edge next to the proposed opening will act as a guide for the saw blade. Of course, this edge is made plumb, with level or plumb bob and line. A two-man crosscut saw is used, one man working on the inside and the other outside. The logs are sawed out and the resulting short pieces set aside for later use in blocking up cracks or for other purposes.

Sawed ends of the logs are held by false jambs, which are 2-in. planks somewhat less in width than the average diameter of the logs. The jambs are placed against the log ends, and securely spiked to each log. It is not a bad idea to apply a preservative to the log ends, to counteract decay. Projecting sides of the logs are chopped off at an angle, as shown. Before cutting the opening, measure the width of the window sash or frame, or the door, or door frame, depending on whether a frame is used in addition to that formed by the false jambs, and then add to it the combined thickness of the jambs.

Perhaps you are asking why short logs are not used in the first place, and fitted against the window and door jambs. The answer is that this sometimes is done, but that it is difficult and more laborious. The logs of a given panel must be cut to exactly uniform lengths, and must be placed so that their combined height is the same all the way around, or the wall will have an objectionable appearance. Whole logs must be used above and below the openings, for stability. When short sections are used for paneling between openings, it sometimes is desirable to nail them together at intervals, in addition to the end-nailing to false jambs.

The simplest types of doors and windows are satisfactory for log cabins. Casement windows that swing inward or outward are considered best. It is not difficut to fit these. The sashes are hung from the frames with butt hinges, and are provided with a sliding bar that can be locked to hold them in any position when open. An ordinary desk-lid slide, with a wing nut working on a bolt running upward through the sill, can be used, or a regular window fitting obtained. The sash swings shut against stops that are strips of wood nailed to the frame, and is locked by a suitable catch. Doors are hung almost exactly like casement windows, except that they have no sliding arrangement to lock them in an open position. Screens should be provided over windows and doors to keep out insects. Door and window design and construction are discussed at length in a later chapter.

When laying cabin walls you can fit the logs closely together or leave cracks between them up to 2 in. or so wide. Some builders hew the logs flat on adjacent surfaces, so that they fit together and require very little chinking. The separation between logs is determined by the taper of the logs and by the depth of the corner notches. Also, it is by varying the depth of the notches that the side walls are kept level. Perhaps the best plan, since you are building a real pioneer cabin, is to pay little attention to the width of cracks between the logs, just as long as they do not become too wide; and then fill in the space by one of the various methods of chinking.

Because logs change their positions in settling during the first year or so after the cabin is completed, the matter of chinking or caulking to close openings between them should be delayed as long as possible.

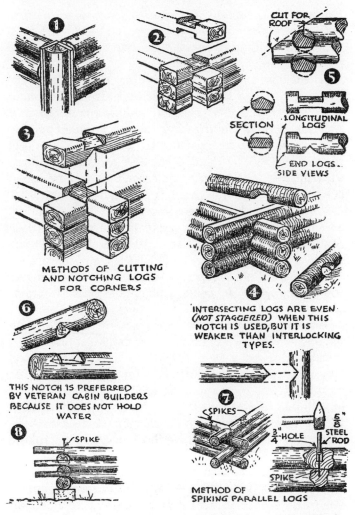

1

2

5 CUT FOR ROOF

SECTION | LONGITUDINAL LOGS

END LOGS. SIDE VIEWS

3

METHODS OF CUTTING AND NOTCHING LOGS FOR CORNERS

4 INTERSECTING LOGS ARE EVEN (*NOT STAGGERED*) WHEN THIS NOTCH IS USED, BUT IT IS WEAKER THAN INTERLOCKING TYPES.

6

THIS NOTCH IS PREFERRED BY VETERAN CABIN BUILDERS BECAUSE IT DOES NOT HOLD WATER

7 SPIKES

$\frac{3}{4}$" HOLE

$\frac{5}{8}$" STEEL ROD

SPIKE

METHOD OF SPIKING PARALLEL LOGS

8 SPIKE

Here are a variety of corners from which to choose. No difficulty will be experienced in making any corner if these directions are followed

However, if the cabin is to be used immediately, you can close up the openings at once, and plan to go over the chinking thoroughly a year later and repeat the process wherever necessary.

A half-dozen methods of chinking and caulking are illustrated. When the openings are narrow, they may be closed by hammering some caulking material into them, as at F in the drawings. A serviceable caulking tool can be made by grinding the end of a 1-in. chisel square. Use this tool and a hammer or mallet to force the caulking material into the cracks. Sphagnum moss, cotton waste, oakum, dried ferns, and various other materials have been used successfully for caulking. Sometimes birds and mice make raids for the purpose of obtaining the moss or ferns for nest-building purposes, when they can reach it. Oakum is a loose fiber obtained from old hemp ropes, and is used extensively for sealing seams in boats. Sphagnum moss is obtainable from florists who use it for packing plants.

When openings between logs are much more than narrow cracks, some method of chinking employing mortar or an equivalent substance is employed. Good clay, properly applied, will last for a dozen years or so. Mix it with water until it is about the consistency of thin putty, and force it into the cracks with a small trowel. Stucco cement, lime mortar, cement mortar, and wood-pulp plaster have been used for chinking cabins. Bagged stucco cement or wood-pulp plaster are merely mixed with water to the desired consistency. The cement is better for the outside. You can make up your own stucco cement by mixing 1 part Portland cement, 3 parts coarse sand, 1 part slaked lime paste, and adding a small amount of hair for binding it together. The hair can be omitted. The mortar whose formula was given in the chapter on foundations can be used.

It is desirable to provide some anchorage for the mortar or whatever else is used. Large-headed nails, driven part-way into the logs as shown at drawing A in the series on chinking methods, serve well. Space them 8 to 12 in. apart. Lathing nails can be used. In B, the outside of the log wall is decorated with small poles nailed in the cracks. The poles serve the purpose also of compressing the mortar behind them and producing a tight joint. This construction might be a bit difficult to re-chink. In method C, a section split from a log is used instead of a round pole. This is a convenient way to use up damaged logs and sections cut from door and window openings. Expanded metal lath strips, nailed in the cracks as shown at D, make a durable support for plaster or mortar. An unusually attractive cabin wall is produced by laying the logs with considerable spacing between them and then filling the spaces with stone slabs imbedded in cement mortar. The stones usually are laid at an angle with the wall. Sandstone is excellent, or field stone broken to the desired size can be used. This construction is shown at E.

Caulking must be done both from the inside and outside. A light-colored material such as lime mortar is desirable for the interior because of its light-reflecting properties, when the log walls are to be left exposed. In addition to caulking or chinking between logs, you will have to plug all openings between the walls and chimney, around the roof, and wherever else insects and undesirable weather can enter.

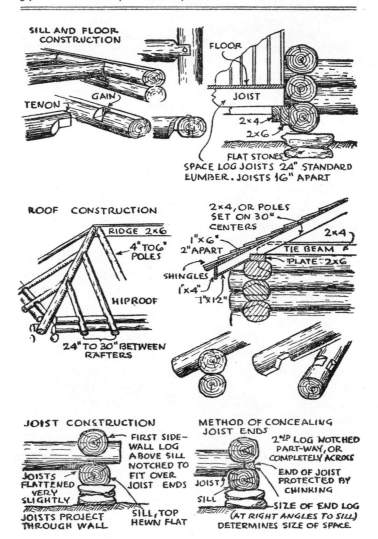

In the illustrations above, directions are given for building a cabin floor, raising a roof, and constructing the joists

Much of the charm of a cabin of real logs, or any
other kind in fact, comes from exercising good taste
in such matters as proportioning, arrangement of windows, arrangement of the logs themselves, and the
color imparted in one way or another.

A low, rambling log cabin is more charming than
one that is high and severe in form. The eaves ought
not be much higher than the top of the door. Porches
and ells and annexes can branch out at the most unexpected places and will add greatly to the appearance
of the structure. Avoid short, stocky construction.
When you build with logs or log substitutes stay away
from structures more than a story high, unless you are
expert at handling architectural details.

Windows can make or ruin a cabin, from the standpoint of appearance. To preserve the rambling effect,
they should be relatively short and wide. The two-
sash type of window used in ordinary houses is not
always at home in the walls of a log cabin. A casement
window is better. Do not be stingy with windows, but
at the same time exercise some judgment in their use.
Some cabin designs lend themselves to the use of ab-
normally large windows running all the way to the
floor, but such cases are not common. In the matter
of windows perhaps more than anything else, the modern cabin builder should depart from the practices of
his pioneer grandfathers. Builders of yesterday did not
appreciate the value of adequate illumination indoors
as much as it is appreciated today. It is entirely possible to install so many windows in the walls of a
cabin room that, when they are open, the room becomes virtually a porch.

The arrangement of logs, as determined by log sizes,

shapes and the type of corner construction used, is an important factor in the general appearance. It is good practice to use the largest available logs at the bottoms of walls, and gradually decrease their size as the tops are approached.

A variation from usual appearance is produced by combining pole construction with horizontal log arrangement. The panels between windows and doors are formed by logs set vertically, while spaces above and below windows and above doors are filled in with horizontal pieces spiked in place. The effect, when the job is properly done, is pleasing.

From the standpoint of exterior finish, the log-cabin builder has little cause for worry. Perhaps the matter of finishing should be postponed until roofs and floors and porches have been discussed; but finishing operations apply mainly to walls, so they can be considered here.

Logs with the bark left on need no attention other than that which might be necessary from the standpoint of insect-proofing. Peeled or hewn logs can be left to weather naturally, although the application of a stain or other preservative that will darken the wood and at the same time provide protection against decay and insect attack, may be desirable in many cases. Of the three principal materials that might be used, namely paint, stain and creosote, stain is preferable because it is easy to apply, produces less objectionable odor than creosote, and gives a more rustic appearance than paint. Stains containing creosote are available. It is best to treat the logs before they are laid in the walls, so that notches and other areas that later will be concealed can be reached. Stain can be applied to the completed walls with a brush or a spray gun of some sort. A simple preservative for peeled logs consists of 2 parts linseed oil and 1 part turpentine. It darkens the wood somewhat, and causes it to take on a mellower, richer brown color with age.

CHAPTER VI

LOG CABIN FLOORS AND ROOFS

IF YOU do not want a cabin floor that resembles a hammock, or a roof that might be a sieve in disguise, avoid hasty and careless construction when you come to these important parts. Much that is said concerning floors and roofs for log cabins can be applied to other types of cabins, and to lodges, bungalows, tourist homes, and similar structures.

The typical cabin floor consists of tongue-and-groove flooring laid on joists made either of logs or dimensioned lumber 2 in. thick. The installation of log joists is properly a part of sill building, and should be completed before the wall proper is erected. Department of Agriculture suggestions for log joists call for spacing on 2-ft. centers. When this spacing is used, the following sizes are specified for various spans: 12-ft. span, use a log 6 in. in diameter; 16-ft. span, 8-in. log; 20 ft. span, 9- to 10-in. Avoid longer spans if possible, because of the danger of sagging. There will be some natural settling or sagging of the log for any span. Some cabin builders compensate for this by hewing the log on top so that the floor is about 2 in. higher in the center, sloping gradually to the edges at the ends of the joists. Center piers and a beam running the length of the cabin (at right angles to joists) will add rigidity.

Strong construction demands that the joist ends be tied into the sills by proper joints. One of the simplest and strongest methods, and one that was used widely by pioneer builders, is to lay the joist ends on the sills and let them project a few inches beyond the outer wall surface, or until they are even with it. The sill is, of course, hewed flat on top. The bottom part of the joist, where it rests on the sill top, should be hewed just enough to prevent rocking. No more wood than absolutely necessary should be cut away, or there may be danger of splitting. A floor, you know, may be called upon to support a great weight. When log joists are used, the weight of the logs themselves amounts to no small figure. Fasten the joist end to the sill by boring a 1-in. hole through the two parts and driving into it a steel or wood pin; or a 40- or 60-penny spike can be used, the hole being then bored half way through the joist end, and the spike driven the rest of the way with the aid of a steel bar used like a punch.

After all the joists have been fastened to the sills in the manner described, the cabin structure will resemble a grating with the two sills, extending along the longer sides of the cabin, serving as a framework for the cross-bars or joists. The first logs across the cabin ends can be laid either before or after the joists are in place. Usually it is preferable to set the joists first, so that the end logs will not be in the way, if continuous sills are not used.

The diameters of these end logs, together with the type and degree of notching, will determine the space between each sill log and the next side-wall log above it. Usually this space can be made so wide that only a small amount of notching will be necessary along the under side of the second log, at the points where the ends of the sills occur. Chinking, possibly with the use of stones in addition to clay or mortar, will take care of the intervening space. It is not important for the top surface of the joists to be even with the tops of the sills. The joist tops are, however, hewed slightly flat, and all irregularities removed so that the floor boards will lie flat.

If the projecting of joist ends through the cabin walls is not desirable, the construction can be varied enough to overcome this. The method can be as described, with the difference that the joists are cut to such length that their ends will come about midway across the sills. Then the log directly above them is notched only halfway across its diameter—just enough to clear the joists. Subsequent chinking will conceal the ends of joists completely, and protect them from the weather. The notching of the top logs can be done with a 2-in. chisel and mallet or hammer.

A third method of attaching joist logs to sills makes use of a relatively difficult joint in which the ends of the joists are mortised into the sills, as shown in the drawings. Each joist end is cut to form a tenon, and a corresponding notch is made in the sill with a wide chisel. A hole is bored through the end of the tenon and into the sill, to receive a pin. The chief objection to this form of joint, according to veteran cabin builders, is that the forming of the tenon, which reduces the diameter of the log at that point, makes the log weaker and likely to split at the base of the tenon if the load becomes too heavy. Tops of joists are even with the sill tops, in this construction.

The scarcity of logs in some localities, and the fact

that sawed lumber frequently can be obtained cheaper than logs, may make it advisable not to use log joists. Timber joists 2 in. thick and spaced 16 in. apart should, according to government experts, be 2 in. wider than the diameters specified for the logs. It is not necessary to do any notching or make fancy joints to fasten sawed joists to the log sills. Flatten each sill on the inner side as well as on top. Then spike a 2- by 6-in. board to it, extending it for the full length of the wall. The upper edge of this board should be approximately even with the top surface of the sill, although it makes no difference if it is not. Next spike a 2- by 4-in. board to the 2- by 6-in. plank, with the upper edges of the two pieces even. The ends of the joists which are cut to fit snugly between the sides of the logs directly above the sills, rest on the ledge formed by the 2 by 4 and the 2 by 6. Toe-nail the joists to the other planks, and if possible to the logs. Further rigidity is produced by bridging the joists every 8 or 10 ft. of their length. This consists of cutting 1- by 4-in. strips of wood to such length that they will extend from the top edge of one joist to the bottom edge of the next one, the ends resting against the joist sides, where they are held by nails. Two such braces are employed at each point, forming an X. This row of X's extends for the full length of the floor.

Another way of setting dimensioned joists, and a more solid way than that just described, is to notch the sill logs to receive the joist ends, just as if tenoned logs were used. Do not cut tenons on the joists, but let them remain their full diameters and cut away the log above, if necessary. The notches should extend about one-third or half the distance across the sills.

When this construction is employed, the load of the floor bears directly on the sills, instead of being transferred from the joist to the sills through spikes. For this reason, the second method is better than the first even though it does involve additional work. If a boring machine is available, the recesses for the 2-in. timbers can be made quickly with the aid of an auger bit of sufficient width. The so-called 2-in. boards procurable at lumber yards are more nearly 1¾ in. thick, for the dimensions are figured when the lumber is sawed and before it is planed.

After the joists are in place, the walls up and the roof completed, the floor can be laid. You can use standard 1- by 4-in. or random-width 1-in. flooring, tongued and grooved so that the edges fit together snugly. Pine, redwood, cypress, or similar low-cost wood is suitable. The boards are fastened to the joists by driving nails at an angle through the tongued edges. The next board covers the nail head. When log joists are used, an 8-penny flooring brad should be employed. With sawed timber joists, the 6-penny flooring brad is large enough, for there is no sapwood that must be penetrated before the more durable heartwood is reached. The floor can be varnished, either with or without staining; or it can be stained, shellacked, and waxed.

The Roof

The type of roof used on a log cabin is largely a matter of personal choice. It should, however, harmonize with the rustic surroundings. Wood shingles are satisfactory, and will last 15 to 50 years, depending on the wood and climate. They probably are more

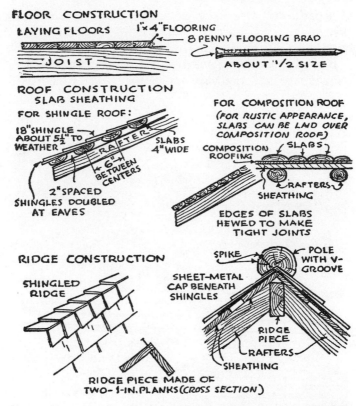

FLOOR CONSTRUCTION

LAYING FLOORS   1"x 4" FLOORING

8 PENNY FLOORING BRAD

JOIST

ABOUT ¹/2 SIZE

ROOF CONSTRUCTION
SLAB SHEATHING

FOR SHINGLE ROOF:

18" SHINGLE
ABOUT 5¼" TO
WEATHER

RAFTER

SLABS
4" WIDE

6"
BETWEEN
CENTERS

2" SPACED
SHINGLES DOUBLED
AT EAVES

FOR COMPOSITION ROOF
(FOR RUSTIC APPEARANCE,
SLABS CAN BE LAID OVER
COMPOSITION ROOF)

COMPOSITION
ROOFING

SLABS

RAFTERS
SHEATHING

EDGES OF SLABS
HEWED TO MAKE
TIGHT JOINTS

RIDGE CONSTRUCTION

SHINGLED
RIDGE

SPIKE

POLE
WITH V-
GROOVE

SHEET-METAL
CAP BENEATH
SHINGLES

RIDGE
PIECE

RAFTERS

SHEATHING

RIDGE PIECE MADE OF
TWO-1-IN. PLANKS (CROSS SECTION)

Floors and roofs give the inexperienced builder much trouble but
this work should be easy if these directions are carefully followed

hazardous, from the fire standpoint, than some other
types. Slabs, strips sawed or split from logs so that
they are flat on one side and curved outward on the
other, can be used, but generally do not give a leak-
proof roof. Composition roofing, composition shingles,
asbestos shingles, and the like can be used, if they are

of a dark, dull color such as brown. Asbestos shingles that simulate weathered wooden ones, even to ridges imitating the raised grain, are available.

But whatever the type of covering, the framework for the roof will not vary much from established de-

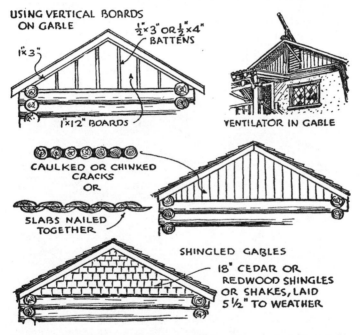

Building and finishing a gable is a simple matter as is indicated by the directions given in this illustration

signs. The plate is the top part of the wall on which the roof rafters rest. This can be a sawed timber or a log. When a straight gabled roof is used—one that looks, in cross section, like the letter V inverted—there may be only two plates, one on each side. When a hip roof—one that resembles a gabled roof with the ends sliced off on an angle—is used, the plates extend along all four walls.

The plates support the rafters, which are notched to fit over them. The tie beam is a pole or 2- by 4-in. plank that ties the ends of the plates together, when but two plates are used. The upper ends of the rafters come together at the ridge piece, a 2- by 6-in. board running the full length of the roof. Rafters are spaced from 16 to 20 in. apart, a closer spacing being used when the roof is likely to have a heavy load of snow to support. The pitch or steepness of the roof is determined by the relative dimensions of the span or horizontal distance across the roof measured above the plates, and the height or distance from the plane of the plates to the ridge piece.

Generally the roof should be one-fourth to one-half pitch. A steeper pitch can be used in regions of heavy snowfall. A roof having a one-fourth pitch has a rise of 6 in. every foot, the height being one fourth the span. When the pitch is one half, the rise is 12 in. every foot, and the span is twice the height.

Cutting rafters demands care, if they are to fit properly. They can be made of either 4- or 6-in. poles or 2- by 4-in. boards. A satisfactory way of notching pole rafters and the plate at the point of intersection is illustrated. When the plate and rafters are 2- by 4-in. timbers, only the rafter is notched, for a maximum depth of half its diameter. Spikes hold the pieces together.

Wide eaves are desirable in log cabins because they keep the log walls dry and add to the rambling appearance of the building. Therefore the rafters generally should project beyond the log walls for a distance of at least a foot.

Upper ends of the rafters are cut on an angle that will permit them to fit solidly against the ridge piece. Whether pole or dimensioned rafters are used, this ridge piece should be of sawed lumber. Rafters are fastened to the ridge piece with nails.

In erecting a roof, cut the ridge piece the same length as the plates, and cut the end rafters (four in number for a straight gable roof) to the proper dimensions. The angles at which the upper and lower ends of the rafters are cut is determined by the pitch desired. A steel square is employed for determining the angle as described in Chapter VIII. Erect the end rafters and fasten them to the ridge piece and plates, which previously should be marked to indicate the positions of other rafters. Then fasten in place the remaining rafters. The roof now is ready for sheathing.

If you have a quantity of slabs cut from logs or can obtain them cheaply at a sawmill, you can use them for sheathing. For a shingle roof there should be spaces between slabs. If the slabs are 4 in. in diameter, they can be spaced 2 in. apart. Lay the slabs with the flat side up (bark side down). If composition roofing requiring a uniform foundation is used, the slabs should fit tightly together at the edges, and some wood should be cut from the edges to eliminate thin parts. Extend the sheathing beyond the gable ends for the required distance. If desired, you can nail the projecting ends of the sheathing to false rafters or boards.

When laying a shingle roof, start with a double course of shingles at the eaves, and then work towards the ridge, all remaining courses being single. Most of each shingle is covered by the ones above it. Satisfactory amounts to expose to the weather are: for shingles 16 in. long, 5 in.; 18-in. shingles, 5½ in., and 24-in. sizes, 10 in. Space shingles ⅛ in., if they are not wet thoroughly just before laying, or dipped in creosote stain. Use copper or zinc-coated nails.

Before laying any kind of roof, cover the ridge and any valleys with painted sheet metal, to reduce possibility of leaking. This metal should extend about 12 in. each way from the joint. The roof covering is laid over it. The ridge of the roof is finished off with a ridge cap of some sort. An excellent cap for a log cabin is made by cutting a V groove along a pole 4 in. or so in diameter. Another way of making a cap is to nail two pieces of 1-in. lumber together to form a trough measuring about 6 in. on a side. Still another way of finishing off the ridge is to lay shingles as indicated in one of the sketches.

There are numerous variations that can be introduced for creating an interesting roof of composition material laid in rolls. One way is to run the strips parallel to the roof ends, that is, from eaves to ridge; and then nail a batten over the seams, after the usual tarred joints have been made. The battens are made by splitting 3-in. poles in halves, or can be sawed strips or sawmill slabs. Other attractive systems can be worked out. As another example, a composition roof can be covered completely with parallel slabs, to give the appearance of the old-fashioned slab roof that, unfortunately, nearly always leaked.

There are a variety of ways to finish the gable ends of log cabins. One is to run the logs all the way to the roof top, cutting the ends to the proper bevel.

Another method that produces a weather-tight and good-looking job is to set 1- by 12-in. boards on end, fastening their lower ends to the tie beam and their upper ends to the end rafters, and then sealing the cracks between edges with battens made of ½- or ¾-in. wood strips about 4 in. wide. Slabs can be used for battens.

The gables can be made of logs or poles set on end and made weather-tight by chinking. A similar effect is produced by slabs in vertical position, nailed either to flat boards or to other slabs set with their flat sides outward and staggered so that joints are covered. Incidentally, this method can be employed for inside partitions.

Shingled gables blend with log construction. Small-sized shingles, such as the 16-in. size with 4½ or 5 in. of wood exposed to the weather, are preferable because the narrow horizontal rows are in harmony with the squatty appearance of the cabin.

A useful feature is a wood ventilator consisting of a series of wood strips set at an angle with lower edges on the outside, installed in the gable. This keeps out rain but admits air. It should be screened on the inside to exclude insects, and provided with a hinged cover so that it can be closed in cold weather.

There are, of course, variations to the method of framing a roof. One way that was employed generations ago, and still is to be found in vacation cabins, is to build the gable ends up to the desired height and shape, and then lay logs or poles parallel to each other and to the eaves. The projecting ends of these poles produce a decorative effect at the gables. Butts and tops are alternated, so that an even construction results. If the poles are laid close together, shingles can be applied directly to them. If composition roofing is used, sheathing must be added. Sometimes these parallel poles or "ribs" are spaced 2 ft. or so apart, and are covered with sheathing running from eaves to ridge. Any type of roof covering can be applied.

A log cabin generally is constructed with ceiling joists or beams. These are logs or dimensioned pieces extending across the cabin, the ends being fastened to the side plates. When the interior is to be finished with ceiling, it makes little difference which kind of ceiling joists are used, because they will be hidden from view. Two-by-fours, their ends spiked to the roof rafters, are commonly employed. When the interior is not to be ceiled, rustic beams extending across the room add much to the appearance. These beams can be massive, and can support vertical logs that extend up to the roof ridge, and which are made rigid with rustic braces set at angles of about 45 degrees to the joists and uprights. Spacing of beams is determined largely by their sizes. Ceiling joists made of 2- by 4-in. lumber generally are on 16-in. centers.

CHAPTER VII

LOG CABIN PORCHES AND INTERIOR DETAILS

A LOG cabin is not complete until it has at least one good-sized porch. Indeed, this is true of any type of vacation structure that is used mostly in summer. While the interior is mainly given over to cooking, sleeping, and congregating about the living-room fireplace on chilly evenings or winter days, the porch will become the most used part of the cabin. In fair weather a hammock, easy chairs, a convenient table, plenty of air and the eternal music of the outdoors lure you and your friends to the porch. For maximum benefit the porch should be screened and protected by curtains against storms. Then it can be used for dining and sleeping purposes, becoming in effect an extra room. And a porch is much cheaper to build than a walled room, no matter whether the cabin is built of logs or shingles.

There are many ways of incorporating a porch into the cabin structure. For instance, if it is desired to have a porch at one of the gable ends of the house, the framework for the porch roof can be made by extending the roof plates and ridge board the required distance, and erecting rafters that continue the roof structure beyond the cabin wall. The inverted V-shaped space beneath the roof generally is left open. If the roof does not project very far, it can be self-

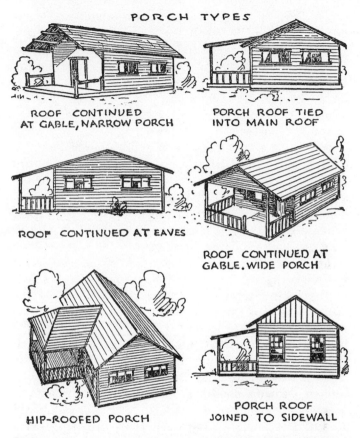

PORCH TYPES

ROOF CONTINUED
AT GABLE, NARROW PORCH

PORCH ROOF TIED
INTO MAIN ROOF

ROOF CONTINUED AT EAVES

ROOF CONTINUED AT
GABLE. WIDE PORCH

HIP-ROOFED PORCH

PORCH ROOF
JOINED TO SIDEWALL

Various types of porches and the manner of building them are
illustrated above and little trouble should be found in following
directions

supporting, no porch posts being required. An interesting and attractive way of making such a roof is to use
longer logs for the upper courses of the sidewalls,
and then install several fairly large logs as ribs in the

roof. These ribs run parallel to the plates and ridge piece. The third sidewall log from the top projects, say, a third of the porch roof extension; the second log from the top, two-thirds of the extension, and the top log all the way across the roof space and for several inches beyond the line where the roof edge will be. The log ribs and ridge piece extend the same degree as the top side-wall log.

When the roof extension over the porch is to be considerable, it is advisable to use corner posts and to close in the gable end of the porch roof, by one of the various methods available; or else make a hip roof. The space above the porch floor generally is not ceiled, because there is no particular advantage in closing it.

When the porch is at the side, so that its roof is virtually or actually a continuation of the eaves, the roof construction will depend somewhat on the height of the cabin proper, and the size and design of the porch. The roof rafters of the cabin can be extended beyond the eaves far enough to provide rafters for the porch roof, if the roof pitch is not great and if the porch roof does not extend out too far. When such a construction would bring the outer edge of the porch roof too near the floor or ground, the roof can be given a smaller pitch, and its rafters tied into the main structure either along the wall below the cabin eaves or in the roof at a point somewhere above the eaves. The latter construction is better when a considerable pitch must be given to the porch roof to provide good drainage. In this case, the porch roof rafters are spiked to those of the main roof. When the cabin is in a region where snowfall is heavy, it is better to use a gable roof, no matter where the porch is situated. A gable roof

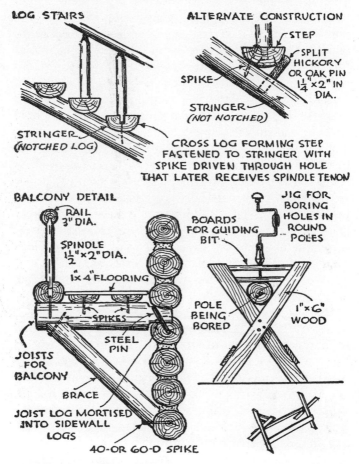

LOG STAIRS

ALTERNATE CONSTRUCTION

STEP

SPLIT HICKORY OR OAK PIN $1\frac{1}{4}" \times 2"$ IN DIA.

SPIKE

STRINGER (NOT NOTCHED)

STRINGER (NOTCHED LOG)

CROSS LOG FORMING STEP FASTENED TO STRINGER WITH SPIKE DRIVEN THROUGH HOLE THAT LATER RECEIVES SPINDLE TENON

BALCONY DETAIL

RAIL 3" DIA.

SPINDLE $1\frac{1}{2}" \times 2"$ DIA.

$1 \times 4"$ FLOORING

SPIKES

JOISTS FOR BALCONY

STEEL PIN

BRACE

JOIST LOG MORTISED INTO SIDEWALL LOGS

40- OR 60-D SPIKE

BOARDS FOR GUIDING BIT

JIG FOR BORING HOLES IN ROUND POLES

POLE BEING BORED

$1" \times 6"$ WOOD

The manner of building stairs and balcony is shown above. Also the best way of holding a log to bore a hole through it is shown

extending from the side of the main roof is tied into it by extending a ridge board and plates outward from the main roof, and erecting rafters in the usual manner.

A rustic construction is almost imperative, if the porch is not to look like something that belongs to another building. Use logs 5 in. or more in diameter for the porch posts, and smaller poles for the porch railing if one is used. Likewise, poles can be employed to build railings along the steps. When it is desired to screen the porch, and open railings are not desirable because screen wire, extended to the floor, is easily damaged by shoes and chair rockers, the porch can be closed in by building a boxing of two rows of slabs staggered and nailed with flat sides in contact, or by setting small poles vertically and close enough together to keep out insects. Building an insect-proof wall of poles is not easy, when a single row is used. A suggested method is to employ two rows of slabs and place a layer of tarred building paper between them. Poles or slabs can be used for closing unsightly spaces beneath porches.

Because a screened-in porch amounts almost to a necessary luxury, set the corner posts and intervening supports in such positions that the spaces between them will take standard-width screen wire tacked to wood frames. Among the standard screen-wire widths are 24, 26, 28, 30, 32, 36, 42 and 48 in. Thus, for 36-in. screen wire, allowing an inch along each edge for frames the space between two posts should be 38, 75, 112 in., etc. These figures allow for an inch between adjacent screen-wire strips, when more than one is used, in addition to the allowance at both sides.

To keep out unwanted wind, sun, and rain, awnings or curtains of some sort are desirable. These can be strips of awning material placed either inside or out. It is easier to make them wind-and water-tight if they

are outside. In that position they also provide protection for the screen wire in winter. A satisfactory
curtain for most purposes consists of a rectangular
piece of awning cloth or canvas with hems at least an
inch wide across the top and bottom. Pass a wooden
strip through the upper hem, and use it as an enclosed
batten for nailing the curtain to the porch frame.
Through the lower hem insert a round wood bar or

A type of porch that is supported by small poles. When screened in,
this provides a large room with the use of little material

metal pipe or rod, to act as a weight and roller. This
bar can be tied down at the ends, when it is desired
to close the area completely. At other times it can be
rolled part-way up and held in position by tie strings
or strips of cloth sewed at intervals along the curtain
edges. When the lower bar is rolled part way up and
held outward from the porch by two supports, the
curtain becomes an effective awning.

Whatever the type of porch, make it as wide as possible, so that there will be room to swing hammocks, serve meals, and move about. So that water will drain off, the porch floor must be sloped slightly. A drop of about 1 in. every 5 or 6 ft., measured from the wall outward, is sufficient. This slope is obtained by running the floor joists parallel to the wall and setting each one slightly lower than the next one towards the wall. Thus for a floor 10 to 12 ft. wide, the outside joist would be 2 in. lower than that next to the house wall.

Run the floor boards across these joists, that is, from the wall outward. If the rainfall is extremely heavy, so that the porch will be wet much of the time, use plain-edged boards, and leave spaces about ⅛ in. wide between them. This prevents water from remaining in the cracks for long periods and rotting the wood. Usually tongue-and-groove flooring, preferably of cypress or redwood for resistance to weather, can be used. When laying the floor, coat the edges of the boards thoroughly with white lead thinned with linseed oil, to produce water-tight joints.

Finish the floor by painting it, or by applying varnish or linseed oil. Paint is probably preferable, but it should be of a color that will harmonize with the remainder of the cabin. In the winter, porch floors catch much of the mud and snow that otherwise would be tracked into the house.

A useful and attractive type of porch consists of a stone-paved terrace overhung by a roof, or else left without overhead protection. Such a terrace can be tucked in at intersecting corners of certain types of log houses. The paving can be of field stones, set in the ground or bonded with mortar.

Interiors

The interior of a log house is likely to present something of a problem. How to finish it? What built-in features to include? How to make the stairs, if any? The fireplace?

Because a log house must go through a settling and drying-out period after it is erected, the applying of finishing material to interior walls should be deferred a year or so, or as long as possible. Chinking done immediately usually has to be repaired the following year. The simplest way of treating interior walls of log cabins is to leave them as they are, with the chinking showing. Bark-covered logs appeal to some persons, while others prefer their logs smooth. If you do not mind the extra labor, you can hew the inner surfaces of the logs flat, to produce even walls. This is done as the logs are put into place.

The particular interior finish you select will depend somewhat upon the uses to which the building is to be put and the tastes of the occupants. If convenience rather than picturesqueness is desired, some sort of smooth wall construction should be employed. Some log cabins are plastered, the plaster being applied to wood or expanded metal lath nailed over the logs. Easier methods are available to the craftsman who is not adept at plastering, or who does not associate plastered walls with rustic cabins. Ordinary tongue-and-groove ceiling boards running vertically can be employed, although there is little to commend this type of covering from the standpoint of beauty. Ordinary ⅜-in. flooring can be used.

A much more pleasing finish is produced with knotty

pine, cypress, redwood, or some kind of plywood material. These materials can be treated in an almost endless variety of ways to make them attractive. They can be worked into all kinds of panels and other

Rustic pillars and braces and an interesting door arrangement make the interior of this cabin attractive

forms. Natural wood surfaces such as these finishing materials produce are much more desirable than the various composition boards. Another useful material is log-cabin siding, made of pine, redwood, pecky cedar or other material. This can be employed in an amazing number of ways to make the cabin interior really charming. Its use is considered more extensively in another chapter.

A knotty-pine finish is easy to produce by anyone capable of handling lumber. At any lumber mill you can purchase pine boards that are full of attractive knots. Select those having round or oval knots, when possible. These boards, simply placed vertically and fastened to the logs with finishing nails whose heads are countersunk, are attractive. Or you can bevel the edges for about $\frac{1}{4}$ in. each way from the corner, and produce a paneled effect. Boards may be of uniform width, say 10 or 12 in., or of random widths. They can be worked into panels and other pleasing variations. When purchasing boards for interior finishing, specify that they be sanded on one side.

In a similar way, cypress, redwood or other inexpensive lumber can be employed. There is available a veneered plywood material that blends excellently with the log-cabin atmosphere. One surface is covered with a veneer of California knotty pine. This plywood can be obtained with the hard parts of the pine grain treated so that they appear as if darkened by natural aging. The purchaser can then use an acid or oil stain or lacquer to color the soft parts of the wood surface any tone desired. He has his choice of several base colors, and of course there is a wide variety of top colors to choose from. By proper blending of colors, any antique or aged effect desired can be reproduced perfectly. Furthermore, finishing costs are lowered because only a coat of the stain and an application of varnish, lacquer sealer, or other protective material is required, instead of the four or more coats usually specified for ordinary wood. Plywood panels generally are obtainable in standard 4- by 8-ft. sizes, and a special 5- by 10-ft. size.

California redwood, an economical lumber obtainable from any lumber dealer, lends itself to interior use because of its natural color, a pleasing reddish hue, and its physical properties. It is close-textured and contains no resin, so that paints applied to it adhere evenly and penetrate readily, with little likelihood of peeling. Although when left in its natural color, redwood is pleasing, it can be stained with any of the standard preparations.

A finish that blends well with log construction, and which can be used for anything from wall surfaces to cabin furniture, is produced by scorching cypress, redwood, or other lumber with a blowtorch and removing the charred wood with a wire brush. This treatment darkens the hard portions of the grain until they range from a rich brown to a black, and darkens the softer portions to a less extent, at the same time giving them an attractive brown color. The burning and brushing can be regulated so that a considerable variety of tones, all in warm brown, can be produced. The grain of the wood becomes three-dimensional, the hard, less charred parts standing out in low relief. This treatment is known as the Sugi process, and is said to have originated in the Orient. It can be used also on pine, cedar, and any other wood that has a grain prominent and differentiated enough to produce the desired finish. It generally is best to apply two coats of floor wax to Sugi wood, to bring out the colors better and to provide a more durable and easily cleaned finish.

These various types of interior finish stray somewhat from the main idea of using materials available in the forest whenever possible. By using, in addition, poles and logs, either peeled or with the bark left on, interesting effects can be obtained. When it is necessary to erect posts and columns for supporting balconies or roofs, these can be of seasoned logs made rigid by knee braces, which are smaller logs set at an angle to the post and extending outward to the surface being supported. The braces can be fastened by mitering and spiking, and perhaps set into shallow recesses cut for them.

Partitions may be built in a variety of ways. Slab or pole construction, as already described for porches and gables, can be employed. Another cheap method is to use wide boards such as 1- by 12-in. knotty pine set vertically, with the cracks between them covered by 2-in. strips or battens from ½ to 1 in. thick, applied to both sides. Still another way of building partitions is to erect 2- by 4-in. studs and cover them with one of the various wall materials, as in ordinary house building.

Although you doubtless will confine yourself to a one-story cabin, you nevertheless may have to build stairs. These may be outside, and lead to porches or doorways; or they may be indoors and lead to balconies. In fact, some cabin builders employ a balcony to provide an ingenious sleeping arrangement or a place for storing suitcases and supplies. By building bunks on balconies that are just high enough above the floor to provide ample clearance, economical use is made of space. A gable roof, especially if it is fairly steep in pitch, provides considerable space above the room. A simple balcony and stairs will make use of some of this otherwise wasted space.

The balcony proper is supported by logs projecting from the wall. When there is a porch or other room on the opposite side of the wall, logs supporting the roof or ceiling can be extended far enough through the wall to provide balcony joists. When this construction is not possible, the joist logs for the balcony can be supported by knee braces set into the wall. Usually these braces will not be in the way. Still another method of supporting the balcony is to drop logs or poles down from the roof rafters or beams extending across the room.

On the projecting log joists, lay slabs or split logs with their curved sides down, where they will be visible from below. An ordinary tongue-and-groove floor can be laid over these.

The stairway leading to the balcony need not be very wide, a clearance of 2 ft. between wall and banister being adequate in most cases. The steps are split logs supported, with the flat sides uppermost, on two strong logs set at the proper angle and notched to receive the curved steps. The railing and spindles are made of small poles, and the supports for the railing are larger logs set on end.

Instead of employing a notched log for a stringer to support the steps, a plain log fitted with strong wooden pins can be used. The pins, which should be from 1 to 2 in. in diameter, and split from oak or hickory or made from peeled poles or branch sections, are driven into holes bored at right angles to the stringer and halfway through it. Steps are kept from shifting in the notch thus formed, by spikes driven through them and into the log below. It is best not to make the rise from step to step more than 8 in.

When using small poles for constructing banisters, furniture, and the like, the usual way of fastening the pieces together is with a type of mortise and tenon joint. The tenon is made by reducing the diameter of the end of the chair rung or spindle until it will fit into an auger hole, an inch or so in diameter, depending on the size of the pieces employed, bored in the piece to which it is to be fastened. A nail, wooden pin, or sometimes glue holds the joint together. Hollow auger bits with adjustable cutting blades can be obtained for forming the tenons quickly. They are held in an ordinary carpenter's brace. A bit for cutting tenons from $\frac{1}{4}$ to $1\frac{1}{4}$ in. in diameter can be purchased for about $2.25.

For holding round poles and logs while they are being bored, a simple boring jig can be made. This works exactly like the V-blocks used by machinists for drilling round shafting. To make the jig, nail pieces of 1- by 6-in. lumber or 2 by 4's together to form X-shaped uprights, and then connect these by boards 3 to 6 ft. long, running horizontally. This produces a jig resembling a saw-horse of a type commonly found near pioneer (and many present-day) woodpiles. The jig might easily be made of 4-in. poles. An added improvement, which is optional, consists of two cross-pieces, placed one about 3 in. above the other, and fastened to one of the X-shaped ends. With the bit to be used for boring the round poles, holes are bored carefully through these pieces, so that they will act as guides for later boring operations.

As already mentioned, the interior of a log cabin is naturally gloomy. So watch your color scheme and try to lighten up the general tone of the room. Make all wall surfaces as light as possible without destroying their harmony with the rest of the structure. In the matter of furniture, table cloths, rugs, curtains, and decorations, you can employ color to produce the necessary cheerfulness, warmth and light-reflecting surfaces. You must, of course, use taste in the employment of color. Even outdoors, color can be added in the form of shingle stain, paint for windows and doors, and gaily-colored flowers in porch boxes, if it is done with taste. Delicate, restrained tones are safest. In fact, if you build a cabin in a National Forest, you will discover that there is a regulation against the use of gaudy colors for anything that is visible from the outside.

Further interior details involve the building and use of furniture, kitchen cabinets, wardrobes, bunks, and fireplaces. Construction of such things is taken up in a special chapter on furniture and other built-in aides to a happy vacation, and a section on fireplaces and chimneys.

CHAPTER VIII

MODERN LOG CABINS

JUST because you cannot obtain a carload of real logs, you need not deny yourself the pleasure that a cabin gives. Manufacturers have modernized the log-cabin idea and made it available to everyone. In fact, the modernized cabin usually is cheaper in the long run than the genuine log variety. But if you insist on logs, and want to avoid much of the heavy work involved in their use, you can purchase ready-cut cabins of real logs of cedar or similar durable wood. These logs are selected for straightness and uniformity of taper, and are notched and otherwise processed in a woodworking mill. For instance, the logs furnished by one company for cabin building are grooved along top and bottom and at ends adjacent to openings, so that splines can be used to produce weather-tight joints without the necessity of chinking.

Such machine-made log cabins are shipped to the purchaser ready-cut throughout, so that all he has to do is put the pieces together in accordance with the plans; or if he desires, he can have the manufacturer take care of the erection as well as the preparation of material. Because of the work involved, the high grade of materials usually employed, and the all-around character of the cabins thus produced, the final cost may be somewhat higher than when ordinary log-cabin

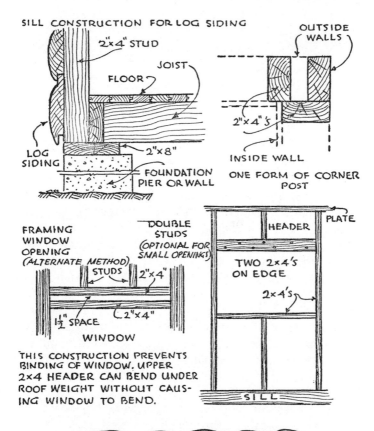

SILL CONSTRUCTION FOR LOG SIDING

2"x4" STUD

JOIST

FLOOR

LOG SIDING

2"x8"

FOUNDATION PIER OR WALL

OUTSIDE WALLS

2"x4"'s

INSIDE WALL

ONE FORM OF CORNER POST

FRAMING WINDOW OPENING (ALTERNATE METHOD)

DOUBLE STUDS (OPTIONAL FOR SMALL OPENINGS)

STUDS

2"x4"

1½" SPACE

2"x4"

WINDOW

THIS CONSTRUCTION PREVENTS BINDING OF WINDOW. UPPER 2x4 HEADER CAN BEND UNDER ROOF WEIGHT WITHOUT CAUSING WINDOW TO BEND.

PLATE

HEADER

TWO 2x4'S ON EDGE

2x4'S

SILL

LOG SIDING IS MADE WITH ROUNDED FACE LIKE WHOLE LOGS AND WITH SHIP LAP EDGE SO THAT EACH PIECE FITS SNUGLY INTO THE NEXT

These illustrations show the proper manner of building sills, walls, and windows when log siding is used in a cabin

building methods are followed or when some of the log substitutes are used.

These log substitutes are siding cut to look like round or hewn logs, and machined so that the edges overlap to produce weather-tight joints. Woods from which they are made vary. Here are some of the log-cabin sidings available at most lumber dealers:

White pine and Norway pine: Outside surface rounded to resemble a peeled pine log. Inside surface flat and smooth, for nailing to studs. Ship-lap joint used at edges, each board overlapping the one below to produce a water-tight joint. Comes in natural pine color, and can be left to weather without further treatment, or covered with shingle stain, clear creosote, or varnish. Available in 2 by 6, 2 by 8 and 2- by 10-in. sizes, and in lengths of 6 to 16 ft.

California Pine and Incense Cedar: Outside surface rounded to resemble peeled logs, or flat and beveled to resemble hewn logs. Pecky cedar siding is made from cedar that contains irregular openings or holes that were formed by fungi while the trees were standing. These holes, which may be several inches long, produce an attractive rustic appearance. Round-log siding of these woods is made in 4-, 6-, 8-, 10- and 12-in. widths, 1½ in. thick; and in 6-, 8- and 10-in. widths, 2⅜ in. thick. Joints usually are single-lap, but can be double-lap in the 10- and 12-in. sizes. Hewed logs siding is produced at the factory with a flat surface, and can be textured with an adz or broadax on the job, to make it look more realistic. It comes in 8- and 10-in. widths, 1½ in. thick, and 8-, 10-, and 12-in. widths, 2⅜ in. thick. California Pine and Incense Cedar can be left to weather naturally, although a preservative consist-

TWO METHODS OF BUILDING CORNERS FOR LOG SIDING

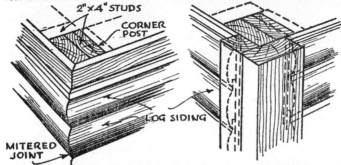

2"x4" STUDS

CORNER POST

LOG SIDING

MITERED JOINT

DOTTED LINES SHOW METHOD OF FRAMING CORNER POST WHEN THE INSIDE IS TO BE SHEATHED, IN WHICH CASE THREE STUDS WILL BE NEEDED INSTEAD OF TWO

ROUNDED CORNER CONSTRUCTION

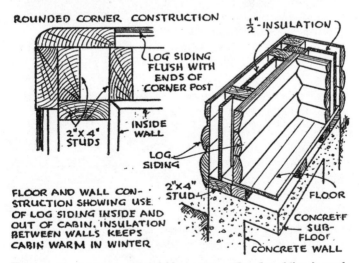

½"-INSULATION

LOG SIDING FLUSH WITH ENDS OF CORNER POST

INSIDE WALL

2"X4" STUDS

LOG SIDING

FLOOR AND WALL CON-STRUCTION SHOWING USE OF LOG SIDING INSIDE AND OUT OF CABIN. INSULATION BETWEEN WALLS KEEPS CABIN WARM IN WINTER

2"X4" STUD

FLOOR

CONCRETE SUB-FLOOR

CONCRETE WALL

Here are the best ways of finishing corners when log siding is used. Note also the manner of floor and wall construction

ing of one part turpentine and two parts linseed oil has been suggested by the manufacturer. This is applied with a brush, and it darkens the wood very slightly. Oil stains can be added if desired.

California Redwood: Several types of log-cabin siding made of redwood are available. The natural resistance of this wood to weather, and its pleasing color make it attractive for imitation log cabins and similar

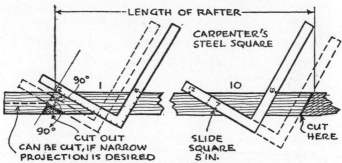

LAYING OUT 1/4-PITCH RAFTER WITH STEEL SQUARE
SPAN = 20 FEET - 10 INCHES

By using a steel square, as shown, you will have no trouble laying out the pitch of rafters for your cabin

structures. The wood is easily worked, and need not be protected with a preservative. It is more resistant to termite invasions than most other materials.

Pecky Cypress: This is a kind of cypress that, like pecky cedar, contains more or less scattered cavities that give it a honeycomb appearance. The cavities are caused by a certain fungus that affects the wood only while the tree is alive. Although the wood may look badly decayed, it nevertheless is sound and strong. The decayed appearance enhances its value for log-cabin

Here is an excellent cabin for hunting or fishing. The screened porch furnishes an extra room (*Courtesy, Page and Hill Co., Minneapolis, Minn.*)

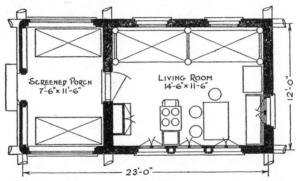

This floor plan of the hunting lodge shown in preceding illustration gives a good idea of the simplicity of its construction

siding. Pecky cypress log siding is made from boards 2 in. thick and 6, 8, and 10 in. wide. Cypress, like redwood, is inherently resistant to decay and weather action. Therefore the log-cabin siding can be left untreated, or it can be stained, treated with the linseed oil-turpentine filler, or otherwise finished.

Log siding, no matter what the wood or the shape,

is applied to a frame of conventional construction. This frame is built mainly of 2-in. lumber 4 in. or more wide. For the average cabin, nothing complicated in the way of a frame is necessary. Simply use the pieces of lumber where they are needed, and make every piece serve a useful purpose. On the other hand, do not skimp on materials when framing the cabin, for the strength and life of any structure depends on the soundness of its frame timbers and the manner in which they are fastened together. Pine or cypress is the usual material employed for frames, although some builders use redwood for the underparts of the structure to lessen decay and damage from termite attacks.

When the foundation has been made ready, your next step is to construct the sills, set the floor joists, and erect the studding, corners, and plates. There are numerous ways of building sills. For the one-story cabin that rests either on piers or a solid foundation, the following simple method will serve:

Determine the size of joists you will have to use. For a 12-ft. span, use a 2- by 8-in. joist; for 16-ft. span, a 2 by 10; for 2c-ft. span, a 2 by 12. It is assumed that you will use only sound boards, free of weak knots, for such load-carrying members as the joists. In fact, sound lumber should be used throughout if the building is expected to give long service. By running a beam down the center of the floor and installing additional piers, the required sizes of joists can be reduced.

The base of the sill is a 2- by 8-in. board laid flat, with its outer edge even with the outside surface of the pier or wall. This is to keep water from running in. It is not a bad idea to cover the top of the foun-

dation with a thin layer of cement mortar and lay
the board in it, to produce a tight joint that will
reduce decay by keeping out water. Before laying this
board permanently, measure in from the outside edge
the width of the 2-by-4 studs, and set on edge a board
that is the same width as the joists to be used. Spike
the two boards together. The resulting construction
looks, in cross section, something like the letter L with
a heel projecting back. The ends of the joist rest on

The sketch at left shows how logs are notched and grooved and put
together in building a corner. At right, how doors and window
frames are fitted snugly into the logs

this heel, and are fastened with spikes to the board
that is resting on edge. Set all joists, and later the
studs, on 16-in. centers.

Studs can be erected one at a time, or assembled
into framework on the ground and erected as a wall
unit. The method depends largely on the number of
men available. The lower ends of the studs rest on the
horizontal 2 by 8, and against the vertical board spiked
to the joist ends. Fasten the studs securely. Upper
ends of studs are fastened to the plate, by spikes driven
through the plate and into the ends of the studs. The

plates may be single or double 2 by 4's. At the corners, 2 by 4's are spiked together to form a corner post. There are several ways of making such a post. If no interior finish, such as veneer paneling, is to be applied, a simple post made by nailing two 2 by 4's together will serve. Where it is desired to form a ledge for nailing finish, three 2 by 4's can be arranged as shown.

The making of window openings is not difficult. Although such openings can be made easier in the frame when it is being assembled on the ground many carpenters prefer to cut out the openings after the studs are up. They say a truer job can be done in that way. This method looks like a waste of material, but the cut-out pieces are used for making cross pieces or headers, and for other purposes. For windows, whose width is not much more than the distance between two or three studs, a single 2 by 4, placed with its widest surface horizontal, will serve as a header. For wider windows, such as the casement types most suitable for low, rambling cabins, it is advisable to place two 2 by 4's on edge, or else use a 2- by 6-in. plank with its face vertical. Remember, the header has to support some of the weight of the roof and other construction above it. It is not a bad idea to double the studs along door and large window openings, for added strength and ease of sash and door operation.

The fastening together of wall framing at the corners consists mainly of tying together the plates. When the building is small and single plates can be used all around for rafter supports, miter joints are made at the corners, the plate ends being spiked to the corner posts. Usually the side plates, which support the rafters, are made by laying one 2 by 4 on the other

Here is a complete one-room cabin with a porch. This is an extremely simple and easily built cabin (*Courtesy, Shevlin Pine Sales Co.*)

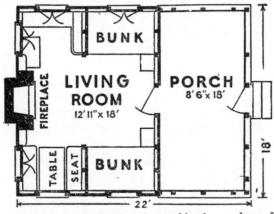

Here is the floor plan of the one-room cabin shown above. Built-in bunks leave a large living room

and nailing them together. When this is done, it is easy to make a lap joint at a corner, the lower half of the doubled plate butting against the end plate, and the upper half overlapping it. For further rigidity, blocks can be nailed in the angle between the corner posts and ends of plates.

The siding can be applied to the frame before the roof framework is erected.

The majority of log houses and their near relatives have simple gable roofs. Framing a roof out of sawed lumber for a cabin using log siding is essentially no different from similar framing for a true log house. Rafters usually are of 2- by 4-in. lumber, and the ridge piece is a 2 by 6.

Cutting rafters seems to be about the most difficult part of roof framing. Suppose, for example, that you want to cut a set of rafters for a quarter pitch roof, one that, in other words, has a rise of 6 in. every foot, or a height equal to one fourth its span measured between the outer edges of the plates.

Look at a steel square when it is placed with the blade or longer part vertical and the tongue or shorter part extended to the left. If you draw a line through the figure 12 on the tongue and the figure 6 on the blade, the pitch of the line will be one-fourth. The pitch, you remember, was defined as the span of a roof divided by its height. The span in this case would be 24 in., since the part of the square from o to 12 in. on the tongue represents only half of the distance across the base of the roof,—half of the span, in other words.

Now to lay out and cut a master rafter that can be used as a pattern for the others: The object is to find the proper length; and to determine bevels for the upper ends, where the rafter meets the one from the opposite side, and the lower end, where it rests on the plate. Assume that the roof span is 20 ft. 10 in., and

This attractive cabin suggests a western ranch house with far-extend-
ing eaves and a pergola porch (*Courtesy, Shevlin Pine Sales Co.*)

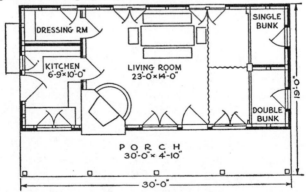

This floor plan of the preceding cottage shows how
the best use is made of all available space (*Courtesy,
Shevlin Pine Sales Co.*)

that you want the rafter to project 12 in. beyond
the plate at the cornice. The pitch, you remember, is
one fourth.

If you want the full width of the rafter to extend for the cornice, it is necessary to cut a notch so that it will fit over the plate. An alternate way is to make the projection one half the width of the rafter. Either way, the first thing is to mark out the notch. At a

Early American history is recalled in this log cabin which is designed along lines similar to those used by the first settlers (*Courtesy, Red River Lumber Co.*)

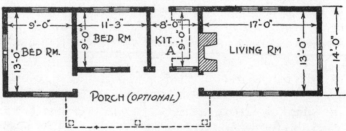

Here is the floor plan of the early American cabin (*Courtesy, Red River Lumber Co.*)

distance of 12 in. from the end of the 2 by 4, make a mark. With the square held so that the tongue is at the bottom and to the left of the blade, place the 12-in. mark on the tongue at the mark you made at the edge of the rafter. This is the starting point. The length of the rafter will be the distance from this point to the point, on the same edge, where it meets the rafter from the opposite side. With the 12-in. mark on the tongue as a pivot, swing the square until the 6-in. mark on the blade is directly over the same edge of the board. The square is now set for the proper pitch. Make a mark along the lower edge of the tongue. Turn the square around and draw a line across the 2 by 4 at right angles to the first line, and intersecting it at the starting point. Mark the mid point on this second line. Again placing the square with the figures 12 and 6 over the edge, move it to the left until the lower edge of the blade intersects the mid point on the second line you drew. From this point to the lower edge of the board along the blade, draw a third line. This line and the one it intersects indicate where the notch should be cut.

Now to lay off the rafter length and mark the upper bevel, or plumb cut: Again place the square with the 12-in. mark of the tongue at the starting point and the 6 of the blade over the edge. Mark the point where the 6 falls, and move the square along until the 12 of the tongue rests at that point. Continue this until the square has been placed at the 12 and 6 marks 10 times along the rafter. (The span was 20 ft. 10 in., half of which, or 10 ft. 5 in., is considered because you are laying off one half of the roof.)

Now for the remaining 5 in. With the square in its 10th position draw a line along the lower edge of the tongue, and make a mark on it exactly 5 in. from the 12-in. mark on the tongue—at the figure 7, in other words. Now slide the square along this line until the figure 12 on the tongue is at the mark. Scribe a line across the 2 by 4 along the lower edge of the blade.

Cut along this line, and cut out the notch at the other end, and your rafter is complete. If a ridge piece comes between the upper ends of rafter pairs, allow for it by deducting half its thickness from the length of each rafter, measured perpendicularly from the beveled end

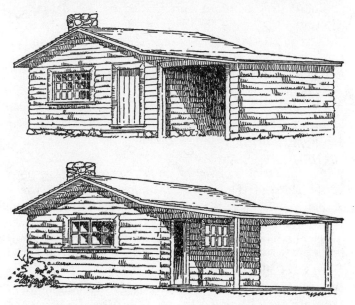

Here are two views of a desirable log cabin. One shows it with an open porch and the other with a one-car garage (*Courtesy, Red River Lumber Co.*)

of the rafter. In the above example, the deduction could be made by subtracting from the 5 in. when marking the upper end bevel.

This system is applicable to all roof pitches. You will note that you do not necessarily determine the actual length of the rafter. Always set the 12-in. mark on the tongue at the starting point. To determine what other number to use for a given pitch, multiply 24 by the pitch. Thus for a one-third pitch, the second number would be 8; for a one-half pitch, 12; for a three-quarter pitch, 18 and a one pitch, 24.

The cutting of more complicated roofs, such as the hip and valley type, involves a somewhat more intricate manipulation of the square. If you tackle such a roof, it is suggested that you consult a capable carpenter or a steel square instruction book.

The rafters are fastened to the ridge piece and the plates with suitable nails. They are further anchored at the lower ends, in most frame structures, by ceiling joists extending across the building from one plate to the other, and nailed to the sides of the rafters. The projecting corners of the joists are cut off to correspond to the slope of the roof. Sheathing boards over which shingles or other roofing materials are placed run across the rafters and project the desired distance at each gable end.

There are various ways of finishing the cornice. For a cabin of almost any type, a simple open cornice is suitable, and possesses the advantage of being cheaper than others. The siding is fitted up over the plate and between the rafters, until it meets the sheathing. A strip can be nailed along the joint, to exclude the weather.

The application of the log-cabin siding probably will prove to be the most interesting part of the cabin construction. The siding, other than being somewhat heavy in some sizes, is easy to handle, cut, and nail when made of any of the woods mentioned. The bottom board is nailed in place first, care being taken that it is straight and level. Then the lower edge of the next board is fitted over it and fastened. This is continued until the wall is covered. The simple window and door frames that you will install can be placed before the siding is put up, the siding boards being cut square at the ends and fitted closely against the

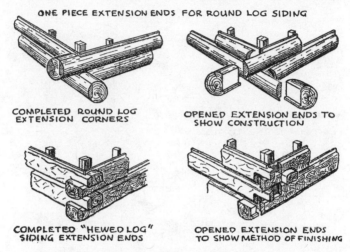

ONE PIECE EXTENSION ENDS FOR ROUND LOG SIDING

COMPLETED ROUND LOG EXTENSION CORNERS

OPENED EXTENSION ENDS TO SHOW CONSTRUCTION

COMPLETED "HEWED LOG" SIDING EXTENSION ENDS

OPENED EXTENSION ENDS TO SHOW METHOD OF FINISHING

In building the cabins shown in the preceding illustration, the corners can be finished as shown here

frames. The siding can be all the same width, or it can be of two or three widths applied in random fashion to simulate real logs.

There are numerous ways of constructing corners. Perhaps the simplest is to make a miter joint where the siding boards come together. When this construction is employed, care must be taken to have boards of the same widths intersect.

A variation of the mitered corner is produced by

butting the ends of the siding against the edges of
boards of the same thickness forming corner posts.

For a wall having high heat-insulating value, log
siding can be used for covering both the inside and
outside walls, and a layer of ½-in. insulating material

LOG SIDING CONSTRUCTION • CORNER DETAILS

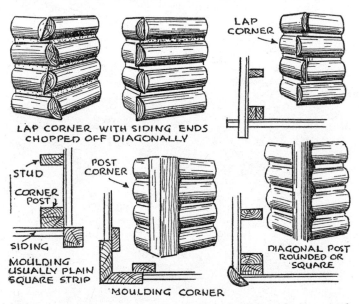

If round log siding is used, the appearance of real logs can be secured
by finishing the corners as shown. Corner construction with hewed
logs is also shown

placed in the space between the studs, midway between
the two walls.

An interesting treatment is to let every alternate
board end at a given corner project beyond the adjacent board on the other wall. The ends are then

chopped off either squarely or at an angle, with a hatchet or ax. The result resembles real log construction.

To provide an even better imitation of real logs, one manufacturer offers extension ends for log siding. When hewed log siding is applied, each board is halved for a distance of several inches from the end, the wood being cut away from the lower half of one board and the upper half of the one from the adjacent wall that intersects it. When the siding is in place, these halved ends project the required distance, which is 2 to 4 in. for hewed logs. To these projections are nailed log extensions of the same length. These extensions come in the form of milled beams that can be cut to any desired length. They are of such shape that, when a section is attached to the siding projection, it completes the log form, producing a strikingly realistic appearance. When the job is neatly done, the seams between siding and projections are hardly noticeable. For round log siding, every alternate board projects 8 to 12 in. for its full width, and the extensions attached.

Another attractive corner is produced by lapping alternate ends of the siding boards, letting the top one project an inch or two beyond the surface of the other. This is an arrangement similar to that employed for chopped ends, but is not quite as rustic. A neat corner is produced by butting the siding ends against a small moulding or square wood bar. A larger post or a real log can be used, the siding ends being butted squarely against its sides, or chamfered roughly with an ax. Another treatment involving a post is to bevel the ends of the siding to an angle of 45 degrees with the wall surface and then fasten a half-round post over the ends.

As already pointed out for real log cabins, the ways of finishing the interior are almost beyond number. Some builders leave the interior unfinished for the first year or two, as a matter of economy. One of the most popular finishes is produced by applying, to the interior walls, log siding like that used outside. The siding can be arranged in rows that come together evenly at the corners, where the ends are cut on a 45-degree miter and fitted together; or the boards can be staggered to simulate real logs, the ends coming together in butt joints made to fit by proper cutting with a scroll saw. Pole-house construction is imitated by running the siding vertically. Incidentally, modernistic interiors have been produced by setting round-log siding vertically and then painting it with white enamel or similar finishing material.

Another popular finish is knotty pine veneer or similar veneered stock. Redwood, pecky cypress, ordinary cypress converted into Sugi wood, knotty pine boards, and a score of other materials treated in a hundred different ways, can be employed. The builder has ample opportunity to exercise his ingenuity in the matter of interior finish. He should, however, avoid materials that fail to harmonize with the rest of the structure, or are otherwise undesirable. Plastered walls are seldom used for vacation cabins because they are costly and seem out of place.

Fancy and extensive interior trim is undesirable. Simple door and window casings or no casings at all, are the rule. The casing of a door, either through a partition or in an outside wall, might well be a hewn beam or made of hewn log siding. When log siding is used for wall covering, no baseboards are necessary, the lower siding strip serving that purpose. Knotty pine boards and plywood usually run all the way to the floor, with only a very narrow mold strip along the intersection. Many of the finishing suggestions made in connection with real log cabins can be applied to the machine-made kind. The same is true of roofs and porches. In fact, it is desirable to work real logs and poles into the log-siding house when such materials are available. Porch posts, projecting rafters and other visible parts of the framework look better in rustic form.

CHAPTER IX

OTHER TYPES OF CABINS

THE log cabin and its modern brother, the frame house with log-cabin siding, by no means enjoy a monopoly among recreational structures. If you have a lake-shore lot, an acre in the woods or mountains, or a site for a tourist camp or other commercial venture, there are many cabin types from which to make a selection. The design and elaborateness of the cabin will be governed largely by the way it is to be used. For instance, a hunting or fishing shack in the woods need not be an elaborate structure, but may be only a wood shell to protect its occupants against storm and the night. On the other hand, a cabin in the woods, which will be used as a year-round retreat for the entire family or even as a permanent residence, will be substantial, weather-tight, and attractive.

From the rural barn, you can get inspiration for a very cheap type of cabin or cottage, yet one that will not be an eyesore and will be staunch and comfortable, if well built. Being "well built" does not mean that it will be costly, but only that its parts are assembled in a workman-like manner. This cabin has simple walls of boards set vertically, the cracks between them covered with battens—strips of wood nailed securely in place.

A framework of 2-in. lumber—2 by 4's for small

structures—is built, to form a support for the wall
boards. This frame is the essence of simplicity, consisting of sills along each wall, corner posts and wall
plates at the top. For added stiffness, 2 by 4's can be
set diagonally, and arranged so that they will miss
window and door openings; or these openings can be
placed where they will not interfere with the braces.
The sills rest on low piers, which can be flat stones laid
on the ground. Joists, massive enough to support the
floor, extend across the structure, and are spaced every
20 in. or so. By generous placing of piers beneath the
floor, 2- by 4-in. joists can be used. They are fastened
to the sills simply by being laid on top of them and
toenailed in place, the ends of the joists being even
with the outer edges of the sills.

Ordinary sheathing boards 1 in. thick and about 12
in. wide are employed for the walls. They are nailed
to the sills, plates and corner posts. At door and window openings, 2 by 4's are used for framing, to increase the rigidity. After the boards are set in place
and fastened to the frame as firmly as possible, the
cracks are covered on the outside, and on the inside
as well if desired, with battens or strips 3 or 4 in. wide
and ½ to 1 in. thick.

As for the roof, it can be of the gable type already
described, or a simple shed roof made by laying the
2- by 4-in. rafters across the plates and spiking them
in place. The shed roof has to have some pitch, something like a rise of 1 in. per foot, to enable the water
to drain off; so it is necessary to make one of the sidewalls lower than the other, and slope the tops of the
end walls. Composition roll roofing is suitable for such
roofs, and is applied over sheathing made of the same

kinds of boards that were used for the walls. Windows of the casement type, swinging inward or outward, are easy to make. Simply set the sash in a frame made of 2- by 4-in. boards, hinging it at one side and providing a fastener at the other, and nail stops all around, to keep the weather out. Slope the sill—the lower part of the window frame—downward, so that water will not stand on it. The door frame can be made of 2 by 4's or 2 by 6's, suitable stops being provided. At the outside wall corners, two battens of different widths should be nailed together to form a trough-like covering, and placed so that the joint between boards is covered by the wider batten.

"Such a cabin would be an eyesore," you may exclaim.

True, there are thousands of such buildings that are most objectionable eyesores. The reason is not primarily with the method of construction, but with the general state of disrepair, the lack of paint or other decorative material, and junky surroundings. By judicious use of paints or stains, you can employ the board-and-batten arrangement as the basis of an interesting wall design. For instance, the boards may be painted a light buff, the battens, window frames, window sash, and door frames a rich brown, and a dark brown roof installed. Another combination would be light green or straw-colored boards with dark green battens and trim and brown roof. Still another combination particularly for a lake-shore cottage, would be white boards and blue battens and trim, with a brown or red roof. In the woods, various tones of brown, in stain or paint, can be used all around.

Additional improvements in appearance can be made

by adding a stone or brick outside chimney, and by judicious use of shrubs, vines, and flowers about the structure. In fact, by exercising a little care, this simple board-and-batten cabin can be made charming and livable. The matter of interior finish and arrangement is one that can be settled according to personal tastes.

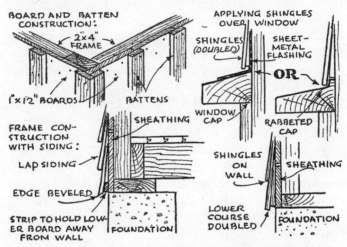

These illustrations show various ways of finishing the walls of a cabin that is not built of logs

With a conventional wood frame, such as that described in the chapter on log-siding cabins, as a starting point, numerous effects can be obtained simply by selection of different outside wall and roof coverings. The builder has at his disposal a variety of wall finishes including ordinary clapboards, drop siding, shingles, shakes, and composition materials made to imitate bricks or shingles.

The terms applied to various types of siding vary

somewhat with locality. In some parts of the country a "clapboard" is something that is used to cover outside walls, corresponding to the weatherboarding or siding of other localities; to old-time cabin builders the clapboard is an overgrown shingle split from logs 24 to 36 in. long and used mainly to cover roofs; while the modern term for this split board is "shake." Some persons think that a shake is the same as a shingle, but it is not. There is a difference in size and method of laying, as will be shown presently.

The application of weatherboarding to outside wall surfaces involves a few simple tricks that every builder should know. Whether the siding is applied directly to the studs, whether building paper is used beneath it to increase weather resistance, or whether the framework is first sheathed with 1-in. boards of pine or other cheap wood, and the paper is used between the sheathing and siding or sheathing and studs, are matters to be determined by available funds, the degree of weather resistance required, and the type of interior finish.

Assume, for the time being, that the cabin is to be used in winter as well as summer, and that maximum weather protection is required. The outside surfaces of the studs will be covered with the sheathing boards, placed either horizontally or diagonally, with very narrow cracks or none at all left between them. Opinions differ as to whether there is any particular advantage in running the sheathing diagonally. Some builders claim that it gives a stiffer structure. At any rate, it is slightly more costly, for some wood and time are lost in cutting diagonal ends.

After the sheathing is in place, a strip of building

paper is run horizontally along the bottom of the wall, and tacked so that it will remain in place while the boards are being applied.

For utmost protection against weather and consequent rotting of sills, a water table is desirable. This is a construction along the lowest edge of the outside finish, for the purpose of diverting water away from

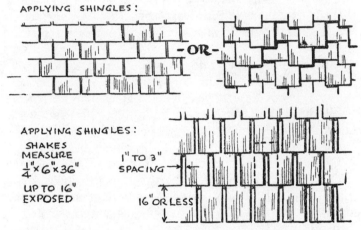

Shingles should be laid as shown with no more than sixteen inches to the weather

the boundary between foundation and sill. A simple way is to tilt the lower edge of the first weather-boarding piece outward an inch or so, and block under it with a flat board whose upper edge may be beveled. Another strip is placed beneath the siding, near the edge, to seal the triangular opening created. In most cases, the construction of an elaborate water table can be omitted without causing trouble for many years. It is a good idea to bevel the lower edge of the first board, so that the outer corner is sharp, permitting water to drip from it. Place the board so that the edge extends slightly below the bottom of the sill.

When lap siding is used, the amount of board width exposed to the weather can be varied. This permits the pieces to be spaced so that it will not be necessary to cut the siding below windows. Tongue-and-groove weatherboarding cannot be varied in this way. Corner boards may be used with weatherboarding, or the ends mitered and butted, with perhaps a protective metal cap added.

Shingles are popular for covering the outside walls of cabins, cottages, bungalows, and lodges because of the variety of decorative effects that can be obtained with them. They are not difficult to apply and last a long time. Because they can be stained almost any color, shingles are at home in the city, at the sea or lake shore, in the mountains, or deep in the forest. Shingles, when laid properly, are better heat insulators than weatherboarding. There is not a great deal of difference between the cost of shingles and of weatherboarding.

Shingles applied to sidewalls can have more area exposed to the weather than when they are used on roofs because water will drain off easier. A less expensive grade of shingles will serve for walls than for roofs. Otherwise, there is little difference in the methods of applying them.

Shingles are obtainable in various sizes, the standard including 16- 18- and 24-in. lengths. The 18- and 24-in. sizes are commonly used for walls. Shingles 9 in. or less in width are preferable. If wider, they should be split. There are no set rules for determining the amount to leave exposed to the weather. Generally, for roofs, the 16-in. shingles are laid with 5 in. to the weather; 18-in. shingles with $5\frac{1}{2}$ in., and 24-in. shingles with 10 in. On walls, the exposure can be an inch or so greater, for a given size.

If a water table is used at the bottom of the wall, the lower course of shingles is forced outward at the bottom by wood strips. Thus the shingles are slightly curved, throwing the water outward away from the foundation. Generally a water table is not used. In either case the lower course of shingles is doubled. This makes it possible to use the faulty shingles that will be found in almost every lot. The top layer of the first course can be set a fraction of an inch lower, so that their bottom edges will project enough to hasten the escape of water.

In order to produce even rows, a straight-edge is employed. When the first course is being started, shingles are tacked in place at the ends. Then the straight edge is placed against their lower edges and fastened temporarily. Subsequent shingles are placed with their butts or thicker ends resting on the straight edge. The straight edge is moved upward, being kept level, for successive courses. If desired, a line drawn taut can be employed instead.

As with lap or clapboard siding, the kind that does not have tongues and grooves, shingle exposure can be varied so that the courses will be even with windows at bottom and top. Of course, it will be necessary to cut off some of the shingles when a window is reached, but the pieces can be used above it. The window cap generally is rabbeted so that a ledge projects upward for $\frac{1}{4}$ in. or more to hold the shingles outward from the wall the necessary distance. Double the shingles above doors and windows. Fasten shingles with zinc-coated or copper 3- or 4-penny shingle nails, driven so that their heads will be covered by the layer above.

At the corners, the shingles can be extended until those on one surface overlap the edges of those on the other surfaces. The over-lapping shingles are trimmed to conform to the other wall surface, with a knife or hatchet. Corner boards can be used, if desired, to produce a trimmed appearance. The boards are set in place over the sheathing, and the shingles butted snugly against them.

The common way of applying shingles is to have their exposed ends form even horizontal rows. They are, of course, staggered so that each shingle covers the joint between two in the next lower course. Variations in the arrangement can be introduced. One way is to set every alternate shingle in a given course a fraction of an inch higher than the others in the same course. A saw-toothed effect is produced, which is less monotonous than orderly lines.

Shingles are made from woods that possess natural resistance to weather. Furthermore, they usually are treated with a creosote stain to increase their life. Ordinarily a shingled roof or sidewall will last from 12 to 15 years, with the sidewall probably giving longer service than the roof. Redwood shingles have been used continuously, without preservatives, for over 50 years.

The woods most generally employed for shingles include cypress, redwood, and western red cedar. Incidentally, these woods are used widely for weatherboarding, with spruce, white pine, fir, and hemlock increasing the list in some sections.

Shakes are essentially overgrown shingles used for roof and sidewall covering. The California Redwood Association has given suggestions for making shakes from redwood. This material is particularly suitable for such uses because it contains no tar or pitch, is straight-grained, and is naturally resistant to decay and insects. Shakes may be made of redwood by sawing or splitting. Special splitting tools having long cutting edges are used. The standard size is 36 in. long, 6 in. wide and ¼ in. thick. A standard bundle contains 25 shakes of this size. They are laid generally with 14 in. exposed to the weather, which produces high heat-insulation value. There is no strict rule for amount of exposure. No. 1 clear vertical grain redwood is the grade frequently employed for shake making.

In applying shakes, set them from 1 to 3 in. apart. This differs from shingle-laying practice, where the pieces are placed closely together. Do not use ordinary iron or blue lath nails for applying shakes. Zinc-coated or hot-dipped galvanized nails are recommended. Use the 4-penny shingle-nail size, two nails per shake.

The number of shakes required for a square (100 sq. ft.) of surface varies with the spacing and exposure. Some values are given by the California Redwood Association as follows:

Exposure to weather	1 in. spacing	2 in. spacing	3 in. spacing
12 in.	172	150	133
14 in.	147	129	113
16 in.	130	113	100

At 2 nails per shake, the number can be determined easily. The nails will run from 250 to 275 per lb.

Of much interest to the prospective cabin owner who does not want to spend much time and effort in playing the part of carpenter or contractor, there are available sectional and pre-cut buildings of types and sizes to meet every vacation need. The sectional house is relatively new, but already is available in numerous localities. Lumber companies and manufacturers are developing the idea because, as they see it, the sectional house will tap a large market that otherwise would not be active.

A sectional building is one that is made and assembled, as far as practicable, in a factory. Wall panels or entire walls, depending on the size of the structure, are built with modern machinery and under favorable shop conditions. These panels contain the necessary window and door openings. When the customer signs on the dotted line, a set of panels, together with other essential parts, are shipped to the building site, where they are set in place and fastened with bolts. The customer buys only the materials that are actually used.

The pre-cut building idea has been applied extensively to inexpensive cabins, cottages, garages, and the like. The sills, rafters, joists, and other essential framing parts are cut to size and shape in a factory, numbered and shipped to the purchaser together with the proper amount of roofing material, weatherboarding, hardware, nails, and paint. Putting up a pre-cut building consists mainly of following directions and driving nails or tightening bolts. For the man who wants to economize on tools and time the pre-cut idea is valuable. Futhermore, waste of material on the job is eliminated, and unskilled or semi-skilled labor is satisfactory.

Modernized log cabins, using log siding, are available in pre-cut form. The builder does not have to worry about getting the rafters cut properly or the sills set correctly, for such parts come ready to install. An idea of the cost of such a structure can be gathered from the fact that a simple one-room cabin about the size of a garage—in fact, it can be used for housing a car—costs about $180, while a five-room cabin with numerous interesting features sells for slightly more than $1,000.

Sectional summer cottages, ready to be bolted together with doors and windows already hung in frames, are priced from less than $300 to nearly $500. More substantial pre-cut summer cottages, suitable for use as hunting and fishing lodges, lakeside or seashore bungalows, and similar recreational structures, range in price from about $200 for a simple, one- or two-room type to about $700 for a five-room cottage with generous porch.

One form of sectional cottage is assembled from factory-made units built of standard 1-in. drop siding in short lengths, the ends being fastened by vertical strips of wood arranged so that adjacent sections fit together with a tongue-and-groove joint, something like standard siding or flooring boards placed on end. These strips serve as studs. Sections are of a size that permits them to be handled easily by two men, their width being about 3 ft. and length about 7 ft., the height of the usual cottage wall from sill to wall plate. The sections are fitted together and bolted along sills and plates.

If you are planning a hunting lodge or other outdoor cabin, the sectional idea may appeal to you for several reasons. By buying the sections ready-made you pay only for material used and the labor involved in making the units. By working out your own sectional design and constructing the units where power tools are available, you can eliminate much of the hard work involved in hauling excess lumber and other material to the cabin site, and in working with hand tools. Transportation of material to a remote location, such as a retreat deep in a forest, involves certain difficulties and costs. If these can be lowered by eliminating hauling of waste material, so much the better. A sectional cottage can be put together in a day or so. Prime coats of paint are applied at the shop, so that only one additional painting is necessary after the building is set up.

Of no little importance to many cabin owners, particularly when the cabin is to be used as a hunting or fishing lodge, is the fact that a properly designed sectional structure can be taken apart and transported to another site, with practically no loss of material. Sometimes a cabin site is leased for a few years, or is in a national or state forest where permission to use the ground is granted for specified periods and can be released at any time, with the privilege of moving the cabin or selling it to a new permittee. Of course, the natural human desire for change operates at times to make it desirable to move the vacation home to another lake or woodland spot.

It is possible to design a sectional house so that walls, roof, and floor are in panels that can be taken apart. Generally it would be advisable to cover the roof in the usual manner with composition material that could be cut apart to permit separation of sections.

For instance, each roof section might be covered with roll roofing to the edges, and only the seams subsequently closed by application of a roofing strip cemented in place. It would be an easy matter to remove this strip and replace it after the cabin had been set up in its new location.

Frank P. Cartwright, chief building engineer of the National Lumber Manufacturers Association, has explained a novel idea that can be applied to the summer home perhaps easier than to any other type, although he primarily was interested in developing inexpensive year-round residences. His plan is to build migratory homes that can be hauled from one location to another by a motor truck. The buildings would be designed so that they could be transported along highways and city streets without colliding with lamp posts and road-side signboards and trees.

At first the idea may sound absurd, Mr. Cartwright explains. But consider the modern motor bus and pullman car. Both are designed to move from place to place, and either of them is more complicated in structure than the summer cabin or permanent home would be. So, to borrow an idea from the transportation industry, the builder of a migratory cottage might construct a framework that resembles the frame of a bus, and which could withstand the twisting and straining incident to moving. He even could build the frame so that the house could be jacked up and equipped with a set of wheels on which to travel to its new location!

Features of the movable cabin include interior finish, if any, flexible enough to withstand vibration and other stresses incident to handling. These conditions are met

by plywood and sawn lumber. The house rests on concrete or stone piers. For winter use, a steam or hot-
water system can be installed, the boiler being on the
main floor, or in an adjacent shed. Water pipes, sewer
pipes and other service lines will be designed so that
they can be disconnected. A fireplace will not be feasible because of the heavy construction required. Cooking can be done on oil, gasoline, or bottled-gas stoves.

Still another building idea that apparently has not
been applied to vacation cabins is the use of rammed
earth for walls. There are standing today rammed-
earth structures of good size that were built years ago.
They are practically as durable as if they were made
of stone or reinforced concrete.

The process of building a rammed-earth cabin would
be about the simplest and cheapest that could be imag-
ined. The building material itself could come from the
cabin site. Any type of earth that, when wet, dries
into firm mud, can be used. Various clays such as the
red clay found in some sections would be excellent.
Straw or other binding material is added to the earth
to hold it together. Water is added until the mixture
is plastic yet very stiff, being moist rather than wet.
Wall forms are built of planks, very much as if concrete were to be poured into them. The earth-and-
straw mixture is dumped into the forms and tamped
firmly into place with a standard iron tamper or a
suitably shaped log. This tamping compacts the earth
until it becomes dense and firm. This process continues
until the wall is built to the desired height.

Window and door frames are set in place as the wall
rises, so that the earth is packed tightly about them.
After the forms are removed, the earthen walls begin

a drying-out and setting process that eventually converts them into something resembling stone. Weather and normal wear and tear are not formidable enemies of the rammed-earth house. Conventional roof construction is used with such a building. The rafters rest on wooden plates laid along the tops of sidewalls, and fastened to timbers imbedded in the walls and extending down to the ground, the walls being thick enough to permit this. Floor joists are set in place in the usual manner, being fastened to sills running along the base of the wall or imbedded part way in it.

CHAPTER X

DOORS, WINDOWS, AND SHUTTERS

ALTHOUGH there is nothing particularly complicated about windows and doors, care should be
taken in installing them because it is at such points
that rain and snow and cold enter and cause discomfort
or damage. It is just as important to have weather-
proof windows in the simple cabin as in the costliest
mansion.

The simplest window imaginable is one that does not
open but consists merely of a sash set permanently
into a wall. However, the fact that cabins, lodges, cottages, and bungalows are fundamentally summer-time
residences, makes the hinged or sliding sash a necessity. For the log cabin, the window sash can be set
into a simple frame made of 2- by 6-in. lumber. The
lower cross member of this frame, or the sill, is sloped
downward so that water will run off. If the window is
to swing outward, the bottom edge of the sash is beveled to correspond to this slope, and a strip of wood,
forming a stop, is nailed firmly along the sill inside
the sash. Likewise, similar stops are used on the side
pieces or jambs and across the top crosspiece or head.
The sash can be hinged either at the top or at one of
the sides, the latter probably being better because the
window glass can be used as a scoop to capture air
currents moving parallel to the wall.

When the sash opens inward, the stops are placed on the outside of it and the bottom edge is not beveled. Instead, the top of the sill, from the front edge of the stop, is planed off so that it is horizontal and not sloping. This permits the sash to swing inward without binding. An alternative construction is to rabbet a groove along the sill and let the sash swing in it, a nailed-on stop in this case not being necessary.

For the somewhat more elaborate construction encountered in framed cabins, a single-sash window frame, like that shown in one of the sketches, can be made. The inside upper edge of the sloping sill is rabbeted to fit the sash, which likewise has a rabbeted edge. The stool is integral with the sill and is so low that its upper surface is slightly below the rabbet. This permits the sash to swing inward. The lower edge of the sash, near the outer surface, should have a groove plowed in it to prevent water from creeping back into the rabbet joint. Note that there is some clearance between the sill top and the grooved surface. The window sash may be swung on hinges at the top or one side. The vertical sides of the sash rest against stops that can be nailed-on strips, or ledges formed by rabbeting out the jambs, the latter method being the better. With this construction, a single-sash window is as storm-proof as more elaborate types.

While the majority of cottages, cabins, and other recreational structures will require casement windows, the type having weighted sliding sashes can be employed in some cases. Window frames for either of these styles should be purchased ready-made. They are cheaper and better than any you could construct. It is a wise plan to obtain the sash before the window openings are framed, so that you will be certain of a good fit.

In order to operate without the aid of a crowbar, a door should be constructed with care from the studding outward. Select the straightest and soundest 2 by 4's out of the lumber shipment and set them aside for use around doors in outside walls and partitions. Double the studs and crosspieces about door openings. The door swings in a frame made generally from ⅞- or 1-in. material. Strips of wood, fastened to the inside surface of the frame, form stops that prevent the door from swinging too far. Sometimes the frame is made of thicker stock and a groove rabbeted out for the door edge, forming a stop.

It is of utmost importance to get the door frame perfectly plumb or nearly so, and to have both sides plumbed to exactly the same degree of accuracy. Then the door will operate without binding. The frame is nailed to the opening in such manner that the outer and inner edges will be flush with the respective wall surfaces if additional trim is to be used. If no trim is to be applied, the frame can project slightly beyond the surfaces. Weatherboarding, shingles, plywood, or other materials used on adjacent surfaces can be butted tightly enough against the frame if care is taken to make cracks a rarity. It is better to use interior and exterior trim with doors, but with inexpensive cottages and similar buildings these can be omitted. Such trim consists of 1-in. boards a few inches wide, nailed around the opening in picture-frame fashion, the crosspiece at the top overlapping the ends of the vertical pieces. There are various ways of arranging the trim, but the simplest is generally the best. Fancy mouldings do little more than catch dirt. For a log cabin, a rugged door frame made from 2-in. material will serve. It can be worked over with an ax or adz or broad chisel, to make it look like a hewn plank. Hang ordinary doors on standard butt hinges and use standard latches and locks for holding them shut.

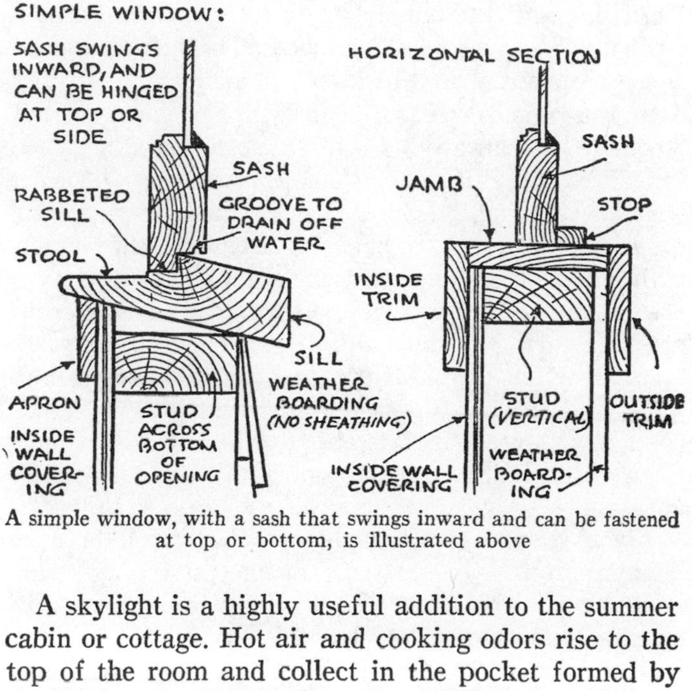

SIMPLE WINDOW:

SASH SWINGS INWARD, AND CAN BE HINGED AT TOP OR SIDE

HORIZONTAL SECTION

SASH

RABBETED SILL

SASH

JAMB

STOP

GROOVE TO DRAIN OFF WATER

STOOL

INSIDE TRIM

SILL

WEATHER BOARDING (NO SHEATHING)

APRON

STUD ACROSS BOTTOM OF OPENING

STUD (VERTICAL)

OUTSIDE TRIM

INSIDE WALL COVERING

INSIDE WALL COVERING

WEATHER BOARDING

A simple window, with a sash that swings inward and can be fastened at top or bottom, is illustrated above

A skylight is a highly useful addition to the summer cabin or cottage. Hot air and cooking odors rise to the top of the room and collect in the pocket formed by the roof and walls. If there is a skylight in the roof, opening it releases these impurities and permits fresh air to enter through ordinary windows and doors. A skylight in the kitchen roof is a source of comfort to the summer cook. Besides improving ventilation, it increases the illumination, a welcome condition in any cabin.

Construction of a skylight is no more difficult than the installation of an ordinary window. In some ways it is simpler. There are several methods of doing the job. One is to cut an opening in the roof somewhat smaller in size than the sash that is to be installed. Then, around this opening, construct a box that extends up from the roof a few inches. The outside dimensions of the box should be about an inch less all around than the outside measurements of the sash. Install metal flashing all around the box, letting it run to the top edges and for several inches each way beneath the roof covering. Hinge the sash to the upper edge of the box in such a way that it projects an inch beyond each side. Along the lower surface of the sash, near the bottom edge, cut a groove to prevent water from creeping back into the joint. If water gets in between the sash and box in sufficient quantity to cause trouble, it generally can be stopped by nailing a strip of sheet copper or painted tinplate about 3 in. wide, all around the sash, so that it projects downward in the form of an apron.

Frame around the skylight opening, when the roof is being erected, in the same manner as around ordinary window openings. Make a light frame to fit the opening and cover it with screen-wire, to keep out insects. The sash can be raised and lowered by a notched bar or rod extending downward through the lower part of this frame, to a point where it can be reached from the inside.

Another way of installing a skylight sash is to mount it flat against the roof and build a box a few inches

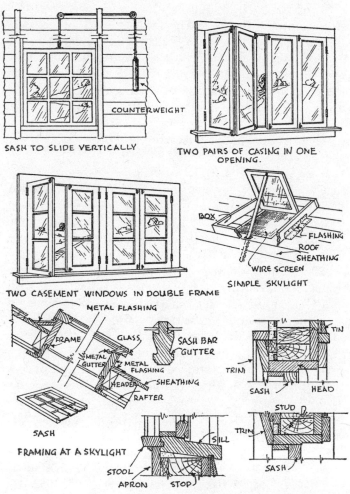

COUNTERWEIGHT

SASH TO SLIDE VERTICALLY

TWO PAIRS OF CASING IN ONE OPENING.

BOX

FLASHING
ROOF
SHEATHING

WIRE SCREEN

SIMPLE SKYLIGHT

TWO CASEMENT WINDOWS IN DOUBLE FRAME

METAL FLASHING

FRAME

GLASS

SASH BAR
GUTTER

METAL
GUTTER

METAL
FLASHING

SHEATHING

HEADER

RAFTER

SASH

FRAMING AT A SKYLIGHT

TIN

TRIM

SASH

HEAD

STUD

TRIM

SASH

STOOL

APRON

STOP

SILL

Easy ways of building windows and skylights are shown here. The detail drawings make clear the manner of construction

high around it, installing flashing as before, and providing drain holes along the lower side.

In the winter, and when the cabin is closed, the skylight should be covered with a board that fits either over the sash or the surrounding box, depending on the type of construction. While ordinary glass can be used, it is safer to employ regular skylight glass, or at least the variety that is reinforced by imbedded wire so that a tree limb or stone falling on it will not shatter it.

It is by straying away from ordinary construction that the builder of a cabin can introduce the interesting details that mark the difference between a charming recreational retreat and an ordinary shack. Among the best places to introduce these little refinements, many of them less costly than ordinary construction, are the doors and windows.

Factory-made doors and window frames and shutters look as out of place in the rustic log cabin as a modernistic chair in an antique shop. You may retort that the constructing of such things is beyond the ability of the average worker in wood. It happens, however, that very interesting doors of the simplest construction imaginable can be made by almost anyone. Also, there are on the market built-up doors, so designed that they will not warp, that are reproductions of rustic doors applicable to log cabins and log-siding houses. These doors are not costly.

The simplest door consists of the required number of boards placed edge to edge and held together by cleats arranged in the shape of a Z. Although such a door has some inherent faults, such as the possibility of twisting and otherwise changing its shape, careful

WINDOW AND DOOR CONSTRUCTION CONTINUED:

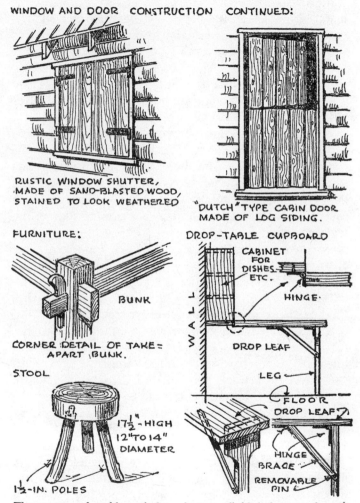

RUSTIC WINDOW SHUTTER,
MADE OF SAND-BLASTED WOOD,
STAINED TO LOOK WEATHERED

"DUTCH" TYPE CABIN DOOR
MADE OF LOG SIDING.

FURNITURE:

DROP-TABLE CUPBOARD

BUNK

CORNER DETAIL OF TAKE=
APART BUNK.

STOOL

17½" - HIGH
12" TO 14"
DIAMETER

1½-IN. POLES

CABINET
FOR
DISHES-
ETC.

HINGE.

WALL

DROP LEAF

LEG

FLOOR

DROP LEAF

HINGE

BRACE

REMOVABLE
PIN

The manner of making window shutters, divided doors, and rustic
furniture is clearly shown in these sketches

workmanship can eliminate much of this. An attractive material is knotty pine boards with their edges slightly chamfered or left square. It is an excellent idea to secure boards with tongues and grooves, so that the joints will be water-tight. If the door is to be used in an outside wall, paint the joints with white lead and oil, being careful to wipe off all excess lead that oozes out, if the door is to be left in a natural finish.

A similar but somewhat more massive door can be made by using log-cabin siding set vertically for the outside, and knotty pine boards on the inside. Joints can be staggered for tightness. When properly done, a door of this construction looks as if it were built of carefully-matched slabs. The Z brace is of course fastened to the inside surface.

For cottages and cabins not of the log-cabin type, ordinary factory-made doors, with or without glass, are suitable. Usually the doors are made about $\frac{1}{8}$ of an in. larger than their listed widths and lengths, so that there will be sufficient wood for fitting.

The so-called Dutch door can be worked into the rustic cabin with ease. This door is in two sections, like barn doors you have seen, so that the upper half can be opened while the lower half remains closed. Such doors are excellent for use in kitchens because they can be opened at the top for ventilation. Doors of this type, as well as of the log-siding and knotty pine board construction, can be purchased ready-made.

For cupboard doors, nothing is simpler to use than plywood $\frac{5}{8}$ to $\frac{3}{4}$ in. thick. This material, made up of five plies of veneer, can be cut out and hung without frames, the edges of the boards being merely planed and sanded smooth. Attractive cupboard and closet doors can be made also of knotty pine, redwood, cypress, cedar, and other attractive woods; or they can be constructed of ordinary flooring or ceiling when appearance is not of prime importance.

To keep out intruders and the weather when the cabin is not used, durable shutters are desirable for all windows. These can consist, for the rustic cabin, of boards weathered naturally or artificially and hung in pairs that swing outward against the side of the structure. White pine, cypress and redwood are among the materials that are suitable. The surface can be wire-brushed or scorched and brushed, to produce a weathered appearance. An attractive shutter is made of log siding arranged either vertically or horizontally. Thus a house covered with log siding can be made to look as if it had no windows at all, simply by closing the shutters. At least one company selling log-cabin materials is offering shutters made of artificially weathered lumber. The boards are sandblasted and stained so that they look as though they had been aged by long exposure to the elements.

Cabins and cottages, finished with shingles or weatherboarding, should be equipped with neat shutters painted in some harmonizing color. Thus a white cottage with buff trim and blue shutters and a rich brown roof would be highly attractive. There is an almost endless variety to the treatment that can be given to shutters to make them attractive. Standard batten-type shutters, the kind having horizontal strips set across them so that air can enter but rain cannot, are suitable, but are not as sturdy as when solid boards are used.

Much charm can be added to rustic doors and to

shutters of all types by careful choice of hardware. Doors made of log siding and knotty boards are striking if hung on massive wrought-iron hinges similar to those seen on old-time houses. A wrought-iron latch to match the hinges is imperative. Some kinds of shutters, such as those made of weathered boards, should be hung on similar wrought hinges. The ingenious craftsman can make these hinges himself, either from bar or strap iron or by re-working large barn-door hinges with a ball-peen hammer and file, to give them an antique finish. There are various devices for fastening shutters back against the outside walls. An S-shaped piece of iron, mounted at the end of an iron rod extending the necessary distance from the wall, was used in Colonial times. This might be adapted to many cottage styles. The S-shaped piece can be turned, like a door button, to fasten or unfasten the shutter.

CHAPTER XI

BUILDING FIREPLACES AND CHIMNEYS

A LOG cabin without a fireplace is as illogical as a rowboat without oars. This applies equally to cabins of real logs or of log siding, and to a lesser degree to other types of construction. As for the less permanent or less pretentious hunting and fishing lodge, lake cottage, or bungalow, cooking and heating equipment frequently involves the installation of safe and efficient smoke pipes, flues, and attendant construction. Many a disastrous fire that interrupted a perfect vacation or week-end recreation period could have been prevented if the builder of the fireplace or chimney had observed some of the simple rules governing such things.

A fireplace in a summer cabin may seem out of place. But there are chilly evenings and damp days to be considered, and nothing is more cheering at such times than an open fire. In winter a good fireplace is an essential part of the cabin. Although from the standpoint of efficiency a fireplace falls far behind various other sources of heat, the fact that the open fire has been a source of safety and comfort to the human race for so many thousands of years gives the fireplace something of the status of an idol or stone god. So if you are planning a cabin, start first with the fireplace, because that probably will be the first thing you will build, along with the foundation piers.

You can build a fireplace and chimney yourself, or hire a mason to do it. Strange as it may seem, few

masons know how to put up a really good fireplace
that will not smoke and a chimney that will not leak.
If you hire the work done, plan to stay on the job
almost constantly, to see that everything goes as it
should. You probably will have long arguments with
the mason to convince him that he should install a
smoke shelf, or place the throat 8 in. above the top of
the fireplace opening, or do something else that good
design calls for. If you do the job yourself, observe
the few rules for proper construction that are given
in this chapter, and you will have little trouble.

The best material for the cabin chimney and fireplace is local stone. Large boulders can be broken to
reveal their inner beauties and to make them convenient to handle. Brick when visible is out of place
in the woods or other rustic setting. Reinforced concrete can be used if the outside is properly textured
and perhaps colored; but a concrete fireplace or outside chimney lacks much of the natural charm of one
built of stone.

From the standpoint of appearance, an outside chimney rising from one end of the cabin is desirable. It
can be reached easily if repair work becomes necessary
in later years. On the other hand an outside chimney is
wasteful of heat and cannot conveniently be made to
serve kitchen stoves and other heating devices. So
the matter of location becomes one largely of personal
choice. Since your goal is not primarily an efficient
heating system but rather one that radiates good cheer
and a certain "atmosphere," the outside chimney probably will win the most votes. Some builders construct
outside barbecue fireplaces at the bases of massive
chimneys, and find them sources of much pleasure.

FIREPLACE AND CHIMNEYS

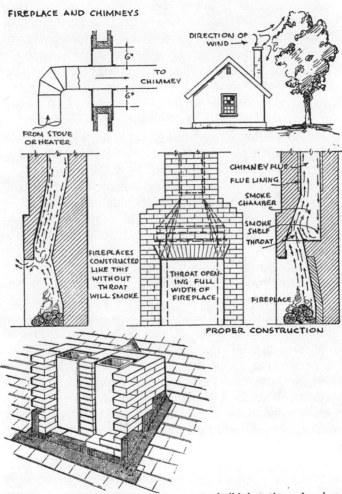

Fireplaces and chimneys are not easy to build but these drawings give you all the facts necessary to construct them correctly

Wherever the location, the chimney must be pro- vided with a substantial foundation. Never support a chimney and fireplace on the wooden framework of a building, or on anything else less secure than the earth itself. Construct a solid footing in a manner similar to that employed for concrete or stone piers. That is, dig a hole a foot or so larger all around than the base of the chimney, fireplace, and hearth com- bined, extending it well below the frost line, and then make a footing of reinforced concrete or stone ma- sonry. Take pains with the footing, for it must support a great weight. An insecure chimney will settle and perhaps sway in the wind, causing damage to the rest of the structure. It generally is the best plan to build the fireplace and chimney first, and to erect the cabin about it.

The chimney-and-fireplace combination consists es- sentially of four parts—the fireplace itself, the throat, smoke chamber, and flue. The shape, construction, and relative dimensions of each of these parts is important.

Determining the size of the fireplace is regulated somewhat by the size and shape of the room. Some builders make the overall width equal to about one- third the longest dimension of the room. Others follow the plan of using a size that merely looks right. The opening should be wider than it is high, or at least square. Never make it higher than wide. A fireplace whose opening is less than 30 in. high is difficult to tend, so that this figure can be taken as a minimum, with the maximum about 40 in. for fireplace openings less than 6 ft. across. The lower opening is less likely to let smoke escape into the room. Other factors de- termining the fireplace size include the type of fuel to be used. Half-length cord-wood requires an opening at least 2½ ft. wide, while if large logs are to be burned the width should be 6 ft. and the depth nearly 30 in. Depth of any fireplace should be 18 in. or more.

While a fireplace hearth may be of solid construction, it is convenient to build an iron grate or ash-dumping device into it at the back, and make a chamber below it into which the ashes fall. When there is no cellar beneath the cabin, the ashes can be removed through an opening built into the outside wall of the chimney and equipped with a tight-fitting iron door. It is best to keep the hearth level with the floor throughout, so that refuse can be swept into it. Some builders follow the plan of elevating the hearth a few inches in the fireplace opening, pointing out that less stooping is required when adding fuel or removing ashes, and that a somewhat better distribution of heat is obtained. Sometimes the hearth curves upward 2 in. or so at the front edge of the fireplace opening, to form an ash pocket. The hearth can be of flat stone or concrete, made as smooth as possible to facilitate tending.

A stone fireplace should be rugged and massive in construction. The distance from the side of the opening to the outer corner of the jamb should be in the proportion of about 16 in. for every 30 in. of opening width. The mantel above the opening can be built as an integral part of the fireplace, with flat stones; or it can be a hewn or split log supported on pegs set in the masonry. Stone chimneys and fireplaces should be at least 1 ft. thick.

Supporting the mass of masonry above the opening is a matter demanding care. When the fireplace is of massive construction, having jambs substantial enough to resist a considerable lateral thrust, an upward-curving arch can be used. Generally, however, a heavy iron beam, preferably of T-shape in cross section, is set above the opening to support the weight. This beam should be sufficiently large to prevent sagging when it becomes hot. The T is placed in an inverted position. Some forms of dampers are built as an integral part of a supporting bar.

The U. S. Department of Agriculture has made a study of proper fireplace construction. Many of the recommendations in this chapter are based on the results of that study. One important point that the government experts stress is proper shape and construction of the fireplace opening.

A fireplace opening can be compared somewhat to a reflector on an automobile headlamp or other source of more or less concentrated light. In the fireplace, heat waves must be reflected by the back and sides of the fireplace into the room. This is the only possible way that a fireplace can heat a room, other than by direct radiation from the fire itself. A fireplace does not circulate heated air as a furnace or stove does. On the contrary, it sucks in cold air, sometimes to the discomfort of occupants of the building, and sends it, together with hot gases, up the flue.

So slope the back of your fireplace forward, beginning the slope about one third the distance from the hearth; and build the sides so that they are straight vertically but slope inward from front to back. Thus the opening is widest at the front, and deepest at the hearth and for a distance upward of about one third the height. Line the sides and back with firebrick laid flat, with their longer edges showing.

By sloping the back surface of the fireplace forward, the opening leading into the smoke chamber and flue is restricted in width. The recommended width for this opening or throat is 4 to 5 in., preferably the smaller figure. It is important that the narrowest part of this opening or throat be 8 in. above the arch or lintel of the fireplace opening, no matter what the diameter or height of the fireplace. Some builders place the throat even with the top edge of the opening, and have a smoky fireplace as a result. It is equally important that the throat extend the full width of the fireplace. Do not start narrowing in the top of the fireplace until after the throat has been reached.

Although a fireplace without a damper will work well if otherwise properly designed, a damper is a highly desirable piece of equipment. Besides providing control over the behavior of the fire by regulating the draft, a damper can be closed when the fireplace is not in use, to keep mosquitoes, flies, birds, squirrels, and other pests from entering the room.

Such fireplace dampers consist of an iron lid hinged at the back of an iron frame that forms the throat. Construction of the throat is simplified because the iron provides a support for the masonry. A damper for a fireplace 36 in. wide or smaller can be purchased for less than five dollars. A handle projects through the front of the fireplace to provide a way of regulating the damper. While the maximum diameter of the throat may be greater than 4 or 5 in., the effective width is regulated by the damper.

Every fireplace should have a smoke shelf and chamber. The shelf is a flat area immediately behind the damper, and extending back until its rear edge is in line with the back of the flue. To understand the necessity for a smoke shelf, it is necessary to observe the action of gas and air currents in a fireplace. Hot gases, sparks, and smoke from the fire rise into the throat of the fireplace because of the difference in air pressure inside and outside the fireplace and chimney. The narrow throat directs these gases along the front surface of the smoke chamber and flue. These gases rise rapidly and cause downward air currents to flow along the back of the flue. If the chimney is improperly constructed, these downward currents will be directed into the throat in such a way that the upward rush of gases and smoke will be checked, and a smoky fireplace will result.

This condition is prevented by making a shelf back of the damper. The downward air currents then strike the shelf and bound forward, intersecting the upward currents at such an angle that they do not cause interference, but are carried back up the chimney. A damper, by creating an upward-sloping path, helps in properly deflecting these downward currents.

A smoke shelf, therefore, is necessary. Its depth is not governed by the size of the fireplace opening, but only by the relative positions of the flue and throat. It should be over 4 in. deep and should extend the full width of the throat.

Between the top of the throat and smoke shelf and the bottom of the flue is a space known as the smoke chamber. It is relatively large in volume, extending as it does over the combined width of the smoke shelf and throat, and the length of these parts. The smoke chamber provides a space in which the downward traveling air currents can expand and thus lessen their speed. It also exerts a cushioning action by providing a pocket to hold the smoke temporarily when gusts of wind blow down the chimney. Without a smoke chamber, such gusts would force smoke into the room. The sidewalls of the fireplace can begin tapering in towards the flue when they reach the base of the smoke chamber; but they should be built straight before that. Although the amount of taper can vary, the Department of Agriculture suggests that the walls be drawn inward 1 ft. for every 18 in. This lessens the friction, as compared with steeper slopes. Finish the walls of the smoke chamber with cement mortar applied at least ½ in. thick, and made smooth to reduce friction.

This cement mortar is of the type that should be used for laying up the fireplace and chimney, with the exception of the firebrick. The government specifications for the mortar are: Mix 9 lbs. of dry hydrated lime with one bag of Portland cement (94 lbs.); then add three times this volume of clean sand and sufficient water to make a smooth-flowing, easily worked paste. Instead of the hydrated lime, ¼ cu. ft. of slaked lime putty can be used. The stones should be wet when mortar is applied. Do not use ordinary lime mortar for fireplaces and chimneys.

The flue is the part of the chimney above the smoke chamber. Good construction demands that it be lined with a smooth-surfaced, fire-resisting material. Commercial flue lining is available in various sizes and shapes. It is set in place as the chimney rises, and filled around with cement. The round form is best because it offers less resistance to spirally moving gases, and can be cleaned easier. Square or oblong flues can be used, but are less desirable than the round ones. Some fireplace builders have employed old hot-water tanks, with their ends cut off, and placed end to end as flue linings. Any metal tube can be used, if good concrete is filled in around it; if the metal rusts or burns out, the concrete surface will serve as a flue.

There should be a correct relation between the area of the flue, measured in cross section, and the area of the fireplace opening. A general rule is to make the flue at least one tenth the area of the opening. This is for round flues. When square ones are used, a somewhat larger flue area is required. If you provide 15 or 16 sq. in. of flue area for every square foot of fireplace opening, you will be safe.

The matter of uniform area throughout is desirable. The area of the throat should be no less than the area of the flue; and the flue area should not decrease at any point from the smoke chamber to the chimney cap. If turns must be made, they should be gradual and the cross-sectional area should be maintained. Do not narrow in the flue opening at the chimney top. There is no advantage to this; in fact, there is a decided disadvantage because such construction decreases the effective flue area throughout.

Only the fireplace gases should be permitted to enter the flue. If the chimney is to be used for conducting smoke and gases away from a cook stove, water heater, incinerator, or other device, provide separate flues, and space them at least 4 in. apart with a solid brick or concrete wall between. A flue with more than one opening will not draw well and is hazardous from a fire standpoint.

It is important that the flue linings be installed so that no leaks will develop at the joints. When two flues run side by side, arrange the sections so that one joint is 8 in. or so above or below the corresponding joint in the other flue. To test a flue for leakage, build a fire of leaves, tar paper, or other smoke-producing material in the fireplace, and then cover the top of the chimney with a wet blanket or piece of canvas. Any leaks will be made visible by escaping smoke. They should be repaired immediately.

Place the top of the chimney where good draft conditions will prevail. It is not good practice to build a chimney near a large tree. When the wind blows over the chimney and strikes the tree, eddy currents will be set up and force the smoke back down the chimney and into the room. Likewise, a near-by hillside may cause downward drafts. These can be counteracted to some extent by building an arch over the chimney top, so that the smoke emerges at the sides. If possible, place the fireplace and chimney on a side where there are no obstructions. The chimney should be at least 2 ft. higher than the roof peak, if the roof is of gable or similar construction; and 3 ft. if a flat type. The higher the chimney, the better the draft. Some chimney experts claim that a chimney should be at least 40 ft. high; but a log cabin with a 40-ft. chimney probably would look more like a misplaced factory.

Whether the chimney is used with a fireplace or other heating equipment, or whether it is of brick, stone, or reinforced concrete, there are various rules of safety that apply. The chimney should be well made, with all joints cemented well, particularly the vertical ones. It should rest on a solid foundation. Wood should not be built into the chimney or come in contact with the outside surface, unless properly insulated. The leaving of a 2-in. space all around a chimney that extends up through a wood structure is advisable. The intervening space can be packed with cinders or other non-rigid, non-burning material that acts as an insulator. At the point where the chimney passes through the roof, install copper flashing. Between the chimney and roof frame should be sufficient space to permit the chimney to settle, expand or contract with temperature changes, and perhaps even sway in the wind, without damaging the building. The copper flashing takes care of these movements and at the same time keeps out the weather. Upper edges of the flashing can be folded over the bricks or stones and imbedded in the mortar for a short distance. Chimneys that are to be surrounded by wood construction can be coated with a layer of cement plaster, to lessen fire danger.

Smoke pipes from stoves can be a real source of trouble or danger when not properly installed. They must be connected into the chimney tightly, running through a thimble of metal or other suitable material. The end of the pipe should be flush with the inner surface of the flue. If it projects beyond that, gases emerging from the pipe will be obstructed by the opposite flue wall. When it is necessary to run a stove pipe from one room through the partition into another room in order to reach the chimney, adequate protection should be provided for the partition. Government suggestions specify a double galvanized iron ventilating thimble at least 12 in. larger than the pipe.

All smoke pipes and flues should be cleaned at least once a year. The occasionally-used cabin chimney will become filled with soot, tree limbs, leaves, and even birds' nests during the periods of idleness. An easy way to clean a fireplace flue is to drop a rope down from the top, tie a bag of leaves or straw on it, and pull the bag up through the flue. A round flue is easier to clean by this method than a square one.

In some large mountain lodges a type of fireplace that is more efficient than the ordinary variety is employed. It is in the center of the room, so that heat radiates from all sides. Smoke is conducted outward by a chimney placed directly above it, and flaring out at the bottom. This cone can be made of metal or masonry, and is supported at the corners by pillars rising from the fireplace hearth. A metal smoke cone probably could be suspended on steel rods, if the roof is sufficiently massive to permit this. Some difficulty might be encountered in building a fireplace of this type so that it will not smoke. But by observing the methods employed for ordinary fireplaces—proper arrangement of the throat, smoke shelf, and smoke chamber—a good job probably can be done. A fireplace open on four sides would be just as heavy as the ordinary type if built of stone masonry; so it would be necessary to provide massive corner pillars to support the chimney, and to make the lintels above the openings sufficiently strong.

But whatever the type of stone fireplace you use, refrain from varnishing the rocks or painting the mortar or otherwise trying to improve on nature. You can, if you wish, plant moss and even small flowering plants in the cracks between stones if they are deep enough; but avoid disturbing the general scheme of things by introducing something that causes discord with the rustic note.

CHAPTER XII

A FEW FURNITURE IDEAS

D O NOT make the mistake of building a cabin and then filling it with cast-off furniture from home. So many cabin owners do this, and then wonder why they do not enjoy their vacations, or why guests fail to exhibit enthusiasm about their woodland retreat. The cabin should be furnished in a manner that is entirely in harmony with the vacation spirit. This does not mean that costly furniture must be purchased. On the contrary, the simplest bunks, chairs, tables, cupboards, and wardrobes will do. In fact simplicity is a necessity: A Louis XIV chair would be as out of place in the average cabin as an elevator.

The most fortunate aspect of furnishing a cabin is that most or all of the furniture can be homemade. Excellence of workmanship is not of vital importance, although it will help. Inexpensive materials can be converted into all sorts of useful pieces of equipment by the average craftsman. Much of the furniture can be of the built-in variety, thus conserving valuable space.

There are two general ideas that can be carried out when furnishing a cabin. One is to design and build furniture that is truly rustic, and possesses nothing of a gaudy or showy nature. Such equipment will be pleasing because it harmonizes with the cabin itself. The other viewpoint is based on the theory that a cabin is essentially lacking in color and other gay features, and that the furniture therefore can be used to liven up the scene—without, of course, showing bad taste. A good plan is to compromise by using rustic pioneer-type furniture and giving the drapes and rugs and cushions the task of introducing color relief.

If you do nothing else during the happy days at your cabin, you will sleep and eat. Therefore bunks and

A pine knotty finish gives the interior of this cabin an attractive appearance (*Courtesy, Shevlin Pine Sales Co.*)

tables and kitchen equipment should be considered from the very beginning. When you plan the cabin, provide ample space for bunks and meal-preparing facilities.

A bunk is a semi-civilized bed. If you are wise, you will insist that it be comfortable, and contain such up-to-date features as a good mattress and springs. Medical experts claim that a good night's sleep is of vital importance to good health. In some cabins, the bunks or beds are made so that they can be folded into or against the wall, to provide more space. However, the value of such an arrangement is doubtful, for there is nothing more convenient than a bed for cat-napping, reading, and otherwise taking it easy during the day. It is difficult to imagine how the space that a bed occupies at night can be used during the day to better advantage than as a general lounging place. So make your bunks solid and permanent.

Bunks can be built-in or separate, movable units. It is largely a matter of personal taste. In either case, it is a good plan to procure the springs first, and then construct the bunk about them. This may not be a scientific way, but for the person who is not familiar with bed construction, it is a satisfactory method. For a built-in bunk, you can construct a simple framework of almost any kind of wood, just so it is strong enough, and make it an integral part of the wall. The frame can be nothing more than a box made of 1-in. lumber, large enough inside to accommodate the springs, and high enough to let you get into or out of it conveniently. Across the boxlike frame place several wooden strips or slats, on which to lay the springs. See that these are level and well fastened.

For a movable bunk, four corner posts measuring 3 or 4 in. square, and side- and end-pieces cut out of 1-in. lumber will serve. Cross slats support the springs and add rigidity. The side- and end-pieces can be attached to the corner posts in several ways. Mortise and tenon joints produce solid corners.

Double-deck bunks are popular in cabins because they save space. The person who is used to sleeping in an upper berth occupies the top bunk, which he reaches by means of a portable ladder or one permanently attached to the bunk. The double decker can be either built-in or movable.

An ingenious two-deck bunk that can be moved or taken apart and stored can be built by the average craftsman. It requires 4 sturdy corner posts of oak,

This rustic washstand is made of slabs with beech poles for legs
(*Courtesy, Shevlin Pine Sales Co.*)

maple, or other durable wood; 4 side-pieces measuring about 1 by 10 in., and 4 end-pieces measuring about 4 by 4 in., the side- and end-pieces being of the proper length to accommodate the springs that will be used. In addition, several slats measuring about 1 by 4 in. will be required, their lengths being determined by the width of the springs.

The corner posts measure about 4 by 4 by 84 in., and should be straight-grained and sound. Oak is an excellent wood to use. With a sharp hatchet go over the pieces until you have produced a hewn surface on them, and rounded all sharp corners. Do the same with the other parts of the bed, and finally remove splinters and rough spots with sandpaper. This texturing can be omitted if desired, but it will add to the appearance of the bunk.

Interlocking mortise and tenon joints, held by wedges, are used at the corners. The construction of such a joint is shown in the sketch. You will notice that the tenon of the crosspiece passes through a hole in the tenon of the sidepiece, and that the crosspiece has a hole in the projecting end of its tenon, through which a hardwood wedge is driven. Although such a joint may look complicated, it is not difficult to form with nothing more than a chisel and mallet. When such joints are used, the bunk is held together firmly, yet can be taken apart in a few minutes simply by knocking out the wedges and pulling the joints apart. The slats rest on strips screwed to the inside surfaces of the crosspieces, near the bottom. Spacers keep the slats in position. Ends of slats are not fastened.

Simple stools are useful, and can be made by anyone who has a saw, hatchet, and auger. One form of stool consists of a slice about 4 in. thick cut from a 10- to 14-in. log. The flat surface forming the stool top is sanded smooth. In the other surface 3 holes are bored to receive the 3 legs that are cut from poles about 1½ in. in diameter. The legs can be anchored in the holes with glue, nails or ½-in. wood dowels driven through holes in the sides. Almost any kind of wood can be used. Beech tree limb sections, with the bark left on, make attractive legs. The stool top should be shellacked or varnished to make it smoother, unless it is finished with a padded cushion of leather, sheepskin, or fabric tacked in place. A simple back can be added to make a chair.

You can build your own furniture from rough stock, as shown, and keep it in harmony with the rest of the cabin (*Courtesy, Shevlin Pine Sales Co.*)

Long, rustic benches will prove popular before the fireplace, at the dining table, on the porch, and in fact almost everywhere else in and about a cabin. Simple benches are constructed like the stool just described, with the exception that the top is a long, wide slab or hewn board. The legs extend all the way through the top, their ends being made flush with the surface. In a similar way, rustic tables can be constructed of slabs or timbers and pole legs. It may be desirable to brace the legs with crosspieces.

Housekeeping in the cabin will be simplified if plenty of cupboards are provided. Everyone knows how to make a simple cupboard. The doors can be constructed in a variety of ways. Knotty pine or cedar lend themselves to the making of attractive doors. Another excellent material is knotty-pine plywood. With it, one-piece cupboard fronts can be made. First cut a piece of plywood to cover the entire cupboard, including the doors and frame or frames about them. Then, with a slender scroll saw, carefully cut out the doors. Hinge them to the surrounding frame, and you have a complete and attractive cupboard front. The plywood is rigid enough not to require auxiliary framing or bracing.

By combining the kitchen table with the cupboard in which dishes and other dining necessities are kept, considerable saving of space is effected. The cupboard itself is conventional, but its door is hinged at the bottom so that, when it is swung downward, it becomes a table. A hinged leg unfolds to support the outer end. This leg can be made non-collapsing by a hinged brace having a hole in the free end through which a pin can be inserted to engage a similar hole in the side of the leg. The leg should be of such length, and the cupboard mounted with its bottom at such height that the distance from floor to table top will be about 30 in.

Another cabin convenience that might be classed as a necessity is a wardrobe. This is essentially a compact clothes closet built of ⅜-in. plywood, ¾- or 1-in. knotty pine or other lumber, and placed near the bunks. It is preferable to a built-in closet because it is cheaper and requires less space. The wardrobe is generally divided into upper and lower parts, closed by separate doors. In the lower part, suits and dresses are suspended on hangers. The shorter upper compartment is for hats and similar articles. A drawer or two for

This table, tipped to show its construction, is made of logs that have been hewn flat

linen is desirable. A depth of 24 in. is sufficient for a wardrobe. Women users of the cabin will appreciate a simple dressing table, with drawers and mirror, built either as part of the wardrobe or placed near it.

You can make a rugged lawn table from logs and slabs. Short sections of small logs or poles are arranged to form X-shaped supports. Across these are horizontal pieces to support the seats. Braces run from the ends of these horizontal pieces to the lower ends of the crossed legs. The top and seats are constructed of logs or slabs hewn flat on top.

There is no end to the things that an ingenious craftsman can find to build for a vacation cabin, once the cabin itself is completed. Chairs, small tables, smoking stands, swings are among the things you may build. Then there are such luxuries as an ice box (when ice is available for it).

However, you may lack the time or inclination to construct your own furniture. You can, then, purchase inexpensive garden and beach furniture almost as cheaply as you could make similar equipment. A few folding deck chairs, a picnic table made of hickory with the bark left on—and much of your furnishing problem is solved, at a cost of less than $10. If the cabin is to be closed for parts of the year, it is not a good idea to fill it with costly equipment, for intruders are always to be expected.

CHAPTER XIII

MODERN CONVENIENCES

THE modern vacation retreat is not, like the pioneer cabin after which it may have been patterned, devoid of all conveniences usually associated with present-day living. Although it is desirable to leave traffic uproar, house-to-house canvassers, and corner lunchrooms far behind, some of the more desirable city conveniences can be enjoyed in the backwoods retreat, particularly those that promote safety and good health.

Too little thought, usually, is given to lighting equipment. Because eye injury does not become visible or otherwise apparent like a broken leg or cauliflower ear, the cabin inhabitant may be doing great damage to his vision by employing makeshift lighting. Reading by a feeble oil lamp or candle flame is, according to vision experts, positively dangerous.

One of the most intense sources of light for the cabin that is not near electric power is a gasoline lantern or lamp using mantles similar to those employed for gas lamps. Such light sources are not costly, and are inexpensive to operate. They are sold widely for farm use. Oil lamps employing similar mantles are available, and are preferable to the ordinary type for reading, working, and other activities involving much use of the eyes.

Bottled gas like that sold for operating rural stoves, or acetylene in convenient containers, can be used as a source of light. Special lighting equipment is available for such fuels.

Frequently the cabin will be situated where electric service is available. This is a desirable condition, and one that should be taken into consideration when the cabin site is being chosen. Besides providing illumination, electricity will do such things as pump water, operate a radio, and cook meals.

If you wire your cabin without the aid of a licensed electrician, make yourself acquainted beforehand with approved methods of installing cable, outlet and connection boxes, switches, sockets, and the like. The fact that the cabin is rustic in construction and finish is no excuse for being careless with the wiring and perhaps causing a costly fire. Conceal all wiring where it will not be visible. If real-log construction is employed, cables can be run parallel to logs and covered with the chinking material. Make sure that they do not run where they will get wet unless they are lead-sheathed. Much of the wiring can be placed beneath the floor, and thus kept out of sight. Provide several convenience outlets in each room and on porches for the connecting of lamps, radios, hotplates, etc.

The Water Supply

For proper safeguarding of health while you and your friends and relatives are occupying your cabin, there must be a safe water supply and a sanitary method of disposing of waste matter. Because a cottage or cabin usually is situated out of reach of city water and sewerage system, methods identical with those applicable to farms can be followed.

It is of utmost importance that an adequate supply of pure water be available. Take this into consideration when selecting a place to build your cabin. Water containing disease germs and animal parasites or their eggs may cause such serious or fatal diseases as typhoid fever, diarrhea, dysentery, or infections of hookworm, tapeworm, seatworm, eelworm, whipworm and roundworm. It is not enough that the water be clear and sparkling. A single drop of such water may contain enough invisible bacteria to cause sickness and death to a thousand persons.

Whatever the source of water it is a good plan to have it tested by a reliable health authority; and then to have repeat tests made at intervals. Local county or state health organizations will do this work, and tell you how to obtain samples. Usually you will be provided with a sterilized bottle in which to collect and transport the water sample.

There are various ways of disinfecting drinking water. However, such methods are not absolutely reliable, especially when performed by the average person. The presence of dissolved mineral salts may offset the disinfecting action to such an extent that you receive no protection. It is only by making an accurate chemical analysis of the water that disinfecting methods can be applied with certainty; and few cabin owners can do this.

Even so, disinfecting water of doubtful purity is better than using it as it is. Among the methods mentioned by the U. S. Department of Agriculture are the following:

1—Boil the water for at least 20 minutes. This is one of the safest methods, but is inconvenient when large quantities are to be treated or when necessary equipment is lacking.

2—Addition of tincture of iodine to the water. Ordinary tincture containing 7 per cent iodine can be obtained at any drug store. Add 1 drop of it to every quart of water (4 drops to the gallon) and let it stand for half an hour before using. There is not enough iodine present to be distasteful or harmful.

3—Use of chlorine tablets sold at drug stores for water purification. Use them according to directions given.

4—Chloride of lime treatment. Dissolve 1 teaspoonful of chloride of lime, sometimes called bleaching powder, in a quart of water. This forms a stock solution that is kept in stoppered bottles marked "Poison." Add 1 teaspoonful of this stock solution to every 2 gallons of water and mix thoroughly. At the end of 30 minutes the water can be used for drinking or cooking purposes. The stock solution loses strength slowly, and must be made up fresh at intervals.

These precautions are not objectionably difficult when the cabin is to be occupied for a few days at a time and a large quantity of drinking water is not necessary. By having the water tested by a health department or chemist, you can determine the effectiveness of the disinfecting process, or procure advice on what method to follow.

Wells and springs are the common sources of water for cabin and camp use. Every precaution should be taken to safeguard these supplies. Open springs are dangerous because the water can become polluted with dust, rain, insects, small animals, and decaying animal and vegetable matter. The springs should be walled and covered, and the water taken out through a pipe. One way is to curb the spring by constructing a rectangular concrete box with walls 5 in. thick, and extending for several feet into the ground where it rests on a loose stone or brick footing. The top is covered by a tight-fitting reinforced concrete lid. Another satisfactory curbing is made by burying two or more lengths of large clay or concrete pipe in the spring. The two upper pipe sections should have T branches in them so that an overflow pipe can be connected to the upper one, and the delivery pipe to the second section. It is best to place the intake end of any delivery pipe some distance below the normal spring surface, and to provide an overflow pipe at the surface.

Wells are of two general types, dug and drilled or driven. Size of a dug well depends on various things such as amount of water required, rate at which it is removed from the well, and speed at which water will enter the hole. A well can be dug with the aid of a block and tackle supported on a tripod tower made from three poles or small logs. One man digs the dirt and loads it into a bucket, which is hauled to the surface by the other man, using the block and tackle. In some soils it is possible to use a centrifugal pump or clam-shell bucket for removing dirt. When wet, unstable soil is encountered, this method can be used, in conjunction with a wood or metal casing that is forced down as the excavation deepens.

Dug wells should be curbed and fitted with a tight concrete capping equipped with a manhole. An efficient curbing is made from large concrete or vitrified sewer pipe, placed with the socket ends uppermost, the joints being cemented securely. At the lower end of the casing, fill about the pipe with stone or gravel, followed by sand. A concrete or clay fill is desirable around the three upper sections. Sewer pipe is considered a cheap and convenient form of curbing material.

The concrete platform is to keep out insects, animals, and surface water. This platform is several inches thick, and cemented firmly to the curbing. It is higher in the center and slopes towards the edges, for quick drainage. The pump pipe and cylinder enter the well through a hole near one side of the circular area directly above the curbing. Bolt the pump securely to the platform, using a gasket for making a tight joint. The bolts can be anchored to the concrete by expansion devices inserted in drilled holes. A better way is to embed the bolts in the concrete when the platform is cast. Ordinary bolts with large washers at their heads buried with the threaded ends projecting, will serve. Beside the pump is a manhole that has a tight-fitting concrete cover. This manhole provides entrance to the well for periodic cleanings.

Before entering a dug well to clean it, lower a lighted candle on a string, or a bird in a cage. If the candle goes out or the bird is overcome, you know that there is no oxygen or that undesirable gases are present, and that the well must be ventilated before it is safe to enter.

Dug wells, when located in safe places and properly walled, are as satisfactory as any. They generally produce softer water than deeper wells, and a greater volume. They are easier to repair if anything goes wrong.

A driven well is merely a pipe forced into the earth until it strikes a water-producing region. Wells can be

driven to depths of 50 to 100 ft. by hand, with an
ordinary sledge hammer or a weight lifted by means of
a pulley and rope and then released. The lower end of
the pipe is equipped with a well point that consists of
a length of pipe fitted with a steel spearhead, and penetrated by rows of holes along the sides. These holes
are covered on the inside with copper screen, to keep
out large particles.

Such well points frequently become clogged, so that
the life of the well may not be more than a few years.
Open-end wells give less trouble from clogging. As the
well is driven, earth enters the open end. This is removed with a sand pump, or washed out by means of
water forced into the casing through a smaller pipe.
Hand-operated pumps suitable for forcing the water
down the pipe are available. It frequently is possible
to assemble a driving or jetting outfit from odds and
ends. Sometimes, when a driven well becomes clogged,
it can be freed by washing out with water forced into
it through a small pipe. If the pump handle snaps
back quickly because of suction, the well probably is
clogged. Slow pumping, to permit the fine material to
dislodge, sometimes will effect a cure.

The location of a well is of utmost importance. It
should never be placed where pollution from outside
privies, garbage pits, surface streams, drainage ditches,
or other sources of filth can drain into it. As a general
rule, the well should be at least 100 ft. from such
places, and never lower than they. A well placed on
ground higher than any of the other camp facilities
may be a bit more difficult to pump and require more
material to reach the water level, but it is less likely
to become polluted. However, the contour of the sur-

face is not a reliable gage, for it is the underground rock and soil strata that determine the flow of surface water that percolates down to them.

In addition to keeping the well away from possible sources of pollution, provide a tight-fitting casing and platform, and keep the ground about it clean. If the water level in the well remains higher than septic tanks and other pollution centers, it is not likely that the well water will be affected. However, in times of drouth or extremely heavy rainfall, the normal water level may fluctuate in such a manner that pollution will flow into the well. The safest plan is to have the water tested at reasonable intervals, after having the well location and surroundings inspected and approved by a local health authority. This may sound like a lot of red tape, but it is nothing compared with the trouble that you would be subjected to by a single case of typhoid fever.

Running water is just as welcome in the vacation cabin as the city home. This is not a costly luxury, and is one that will do much towards improving sanitary conditions. The division of the vacation party that presides over the kitchen will appreciate the convenience of turning a faucet when water is desired, instead of having to pump it by hand and perhaps carry it into the kitchen in a pail.

You can purchase, for a surprisingly small sum, electric- or gasoline-driven pump-and-tank outfits that will assure a constant and reliable water supply. The pump lifts water from a well and forces it into a tank that contains some air. The air is compressed at the closed end of the tank until the desired pressure is reached, when the motor or engine stops automatically.

When a faucet is opened, the compressed air forces the water out through it. Electric pumps start automatically when the pressure drops below a certain point. Gasoline pumps are started by hand when the pressure becomes low.

The installation of pumps, water pipes, and other items of plumbing equipment can be undertaken by the average man. Modern plumbing consists mostly of assembling articles that are purchased ready to put together or install.

Sewage Disposal

Close attention to the facilities provided for disposal of human excrement, garbage, sink drainage, and other waste materials will do much to increase the safety and pleasure of the cabin. The water supply and sewage disposal system should be considered when you plan your cabin, so that one will not interfere with the other.

There is one thing that most persons overlook: No matter what sanitary system you install, you must give it reasonable attention or it may become worse than useless. Periodic cleanings are necessary.

Among the items that are adaptable for summer-home use are various types of privies, septic tank systems, and sink-drainage wastage systems.

A visit to the average summer colony that does not have a sanitary sewer system indicates that there is a desperate need for an authority on the subject of outhouse construction. While the common privy has been made the object of untold quantities of humor, it too often works in league with death. Epidemics of serious

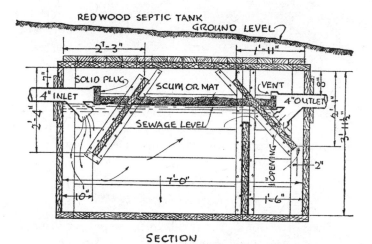

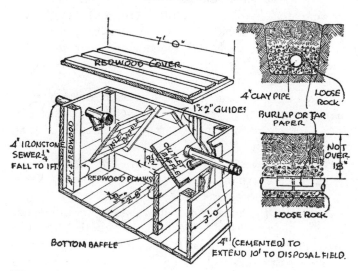

The two sketches above show the details necessary to the construction
of a suitable septic tank

diseases have been traced time and again to insanitary privies.

The U. S. Department of Agriculture has collected and assembled into a booklet a considerable quantity of information on the proper disposal of farm sewage. Since a woodland cabin presents a problem identical

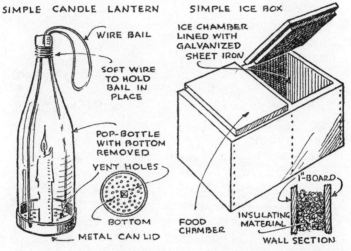

SIMPLE CANDLE LANTERN   SIMPLE ICE BOX

WIRE BAIL

SOFT WIRE
TO HOLD
BAIL IN
PLACE

POP-BOTTLE
WITH BOTTOM
REMOVED

VENT HOLES

BOTTOM

METAL CAN LID

ICE CHAMBER
LINED WITH
GALVANIZED
SHEET IRON

1" BOARD

FOOD
CHAMBER

INSULATING
MATERIAL

WALL SECTION

You can make your own candle lantern and cabin ice box if you follow the directions given above and in the text on page 180

with that involving the farmhouse, the cabin owner will find it worth while to procure this bulletin, as well as others pertaining to related subjects. Farmers' Bulletin No. 1227, pertaining to sewage disposal, can be purchased for 10 cents from the Superintendent of Documents, Washington, D. C. You will find other helpful government publications listed elsewhere in this book.

The outside privy should be located at least 100 ft. from the water supply, and on a lower level. It should be in a concealed spot, camouflaged by bushes, arbors, vines, or other means. Waste matter should not be discharged upon the ground, but should be retained by metal pails, concrete vaults, or chemical tanks.

One of the simplest outdoor privies is the pail type illustrated. Note that considerable effort has been devoted to the providing of proper ventilation, and that all ventilating and lighting openings are screened to prevent insects from entering. The seat, of painted lumber, is hinged so that the metal container can be removed. This container is emptied at frequent intervals, the contents being buried a few inches beneath the ground, in a remote spot where there is no possibility of causing pollution of wells or streams. In the soil, the material decomposes naturally and eventually becomes harmless. Do not use this waste matter for fertilizing gardens or shrubbery. It is a source of danger, and not very efficient as a fertilizer.

A more elaborate arrangement is the vault privy. A water-tight vault of concrete is constructed, and above it a well-ventilated house built. Care must be taken to build the vault and wooden structure so that flies and other insects cannot enter to carry away filth that eventually might reach your table and food. The vault, as shown in the drawing, is shallow and so designed that it can be cleaned regularly.

For indoor installations where sewerage facilities are not available, chemical closets are satisfactory. Various types are on the market. The waste matter is retained in a metal pail or tank, and chemicals added to render it harmless and inoffensive. There is no reliable in-

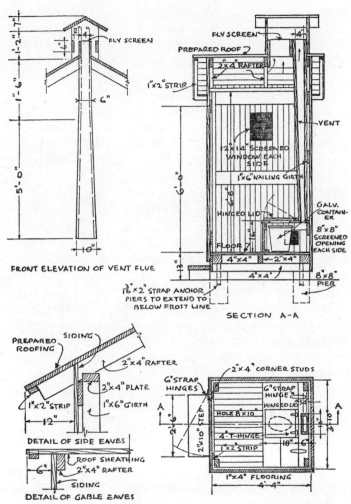

FRONT ELEVATION OF VENT FLUE

FLY SCREEN

2"x4"

6"

6"

6"

5'-0"

10"

FLY SCREEN

4"

PREPARED ROOF

2"x4" RAFTER

1"x2" STRIP

VENT

12"x14" SCREENED WINDOW EACH SIDE

1"x6" NAILING GIRTH

6'-0"

6'-0"

HINGED LID

GALV. CONTAINER

8"x8" SCREENED OPENING EACH SIDE

FLOOR

4"x4"

2"x4"

4"x4"

8"x8" PIER

1½"x2" STRAP ANCHOR PIERS TO EXTEND TO BELOW FROST LINE

SECTION A-A

PREPARED ROOFING

SIDING

2"x4" RAFTER

2"x4" PLATE

1"x6" GIRTH

1"x2" STRIP

12"

DETAIL OF SIDE EAVES

ROOF SHEATHING

2"x4" RAFTER

SIDING

6"

DETAIL OF GABLE EAVES

2"x4" CORNER STUDS

6' STRAP HINGES

6' STRAP HINGE

HINGED LID

HOLE 8x10

4' T-HINGE

1"x2" STRIP

2"x10" STEP

18"

A

A

1"x4" FLOORING

4'-4"

3'-10"

A satisfactory and sanitary privy suitable for a log cabin site is given in these sketches

formation available on the efficiency of such systems, but it is claimed by health authorities that the chemicals, as ordinarily used, often fall far short of producing complete sterilization of the pail or tank contents. Chemical closets have to be emptied at intervals, and the contents buried or otherwise destroyed.

Caustic soda is commonly used in chemical closets. When sufficiently concentrated and mixed well with the contents, it and similar caustic materials dissolve the solid matter and destroy bacteria. Caustic soda costs about 10 cents a pound. Coal-tar products and other disinfectants have been employed in chemical closets. They do not dissolve solid matter, but are good deodorants and germ-killers. It is essential that any of these chemicals be mixed thoroughly with the waste matter. For this reason, some types of chemical closets are equipped with mechanical agitators.

Chemical disinfectants and deodorizers can be used in pail- and vault-type privies. Among those substances that have been employed are quicklime, which gives off heat when in contact with water; chloride of lime; ordinary lime mixed with water (whitewash), and applied frequently to vaults, walls, etc., where it checks bacterial growth; iron sulphate, $\frac{1}{4}$ lb. to one gallon of water, used as a deodorant for drains and vaults. Government sanitary experts recommend that the contents of a privy vault be sprinkled daily with some material that will absorb moisture and odor. Among the materials suggested in addition to some of the above are ashes, sawdust, loose dry soil, charcoal, powdered peat, and ground gypsum.

Drainage from kitchen sinks has to be disposed of in a safe manner, if strictly sanitary conditions are to

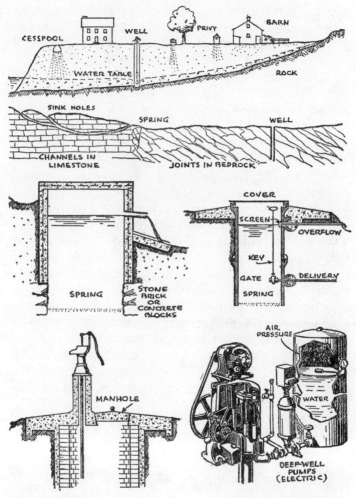

In the illustrations above, the wrong way of disposing of sewage is shown. In this arrangement of well and privy unsanitary conditions are sure to prevail

prevail. One method is to conduct the drainage through well-cemented vitrified tile to a point at least 100 fet. from any well and below it. There the liquid enters a blind drain from which it seeps into a bed of coke, gravel, coarse sand, stones, cinders, slag or broken brick. This bed is 18 in. deep, and covered over with strips of tar paper, a layer of straw, cornstalks, or other material that will keep the foot-thick layer of soil above it from washing down among the loose material. The sink waste is distributed through the bed by a few lengths of tile, laid with open joints and the hubs down hill.

A septic tank system is perhaps the most efficient method of disposing of both sewage and sink drainage, when running water is available. A septic tank is essentially a buried tank of concrete, brick, metal, or wood in which the sewage rests for a day or so while natural action of bacteria converts some of the solid material into liquids and gasses. The liquids drain off into a distribution field and eventually enter the ground, while the gases escape through vents.

Contrary to general belief, a septic tank system is not a complete method of getting rid of sewage. Only a portion of the solid matter is destroyed, and odor is not lacking. The overflow or effluent is highly charged with bacteria and therefore is dangerous if released where it can contaminate wells, springs, or streams.

A septic tank system consists of several parts. The sewage is conducted from water-flushed toilets and sinks and bathtubs through a water-tight sewer made of glazed vitrified sewer pipe, cast-iron soil pipe, or concrete pipe, to the septic tank, which should be at least 50 to 100 ft. from the house. A 5-in. sewer having

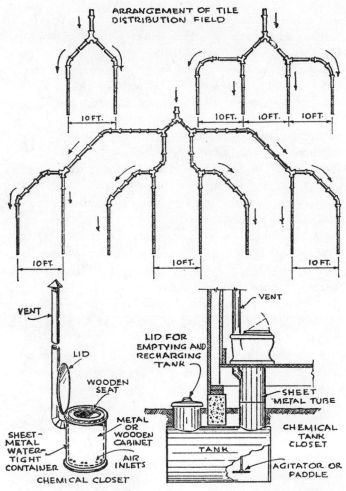

If chemical closets are used, arrangements for the disposition of sewage should be made as shown here

a fall of not less than 1½ ft. for every 100 ft. of length, will serve for most installations.

The septic tank is buried in the ground, either with the top level with the ground surface or 1 to 2 ft. below it, depending on the severity of winter weather in the locality. It is desirable to keep the tank temperature high enough at all times to hasten bacterial growth. The tank, no matter of what it is constructed, should be covered tightly.

There are various designs for septic tanks. All of them consist essentially of a walled vault with an inlet on one side and an outlet on the other, and with baffles to prevent incoming currents from agitating the contents or from escaping immediately through the outlet. Septic tanks made of rust-proof metal can be purchased for about $15. In addition, a grease trap costing less than $10 can be added if desired, to keep kitchen grease from clogging the tank. However, if the cook is careful and disposes of grease with the garbage instead of letting it enter the sink drain, a grease trap can be omitted.

A simple septic tank can be built of brick. A cubical tank 2 ft. by 4 ft., and 5 ft. deep will handle the sewage of a half-dozen persons. The side walls of such a tank are 8 in. thick, the bottom 4 in. thick, and the inlet and outlet pipes arranged so that the liquid level will be 12 in. below the double plank cover. A wood baffle extending for 3 ft. below the level of the tank top, and placed 8 in. in front of the inlet sewer opening, prevents undue stirring of the contents.

Another simple septic tank is made from two 3-ft. lengths of 2-ft. vitrified sewer pipe buried vertically in

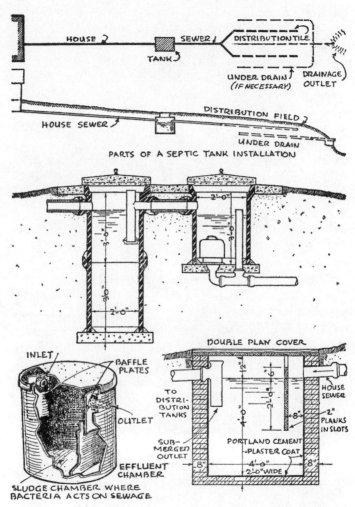

PARTS OF A SEPTIC TANK INSTALLATION

Detailed drawings showing exactly how septic tanks should be installed and maintained to keep them sanitary

the ground, and provided with a concrete bottom and top.

For year-round operation, the Department of Agriculture recommends that a two-chamber tank be installed. One of the chambers is where the sewage settles and undergoes bacterial action, and the other contains an automatic siphon that periodically discharges the effluent into the distribution field. Such siphons are not costly. Intermittent discharge is more desirable than constant wetting of the distribution field. A double septic tank can be built cheaply from 3 lengths of 2-ft. sewer pipe, one of which has double T-branches and another a single T-branch.

Several types of wooden tanks have given satisfactory service. One successful design was worked out by the University of California. Redwood is the material used because of its natural resistance to decay. The construction of such a tank can be undertaken by anyone familiar with tools. It consists of a rectangular redwood tank and a cover made of the same material. Two branched sewer pipe sections 4 in. in diameter are fitted to the tank as shown, the outlet pipe being 1 in. lower than the inlet. Note that the straight end of the inlet pipe is plugged, and that the corresponding end of the outlet is plugged also but has a vent hole at the top. Positions of the three baffles are shown in the drawings. Tanks of this type have been in successful operation for over 10 years. They require cleaning only at intervals of several years.

For a tank of the University of California type, the following materials will be required. Dimensions are exact.

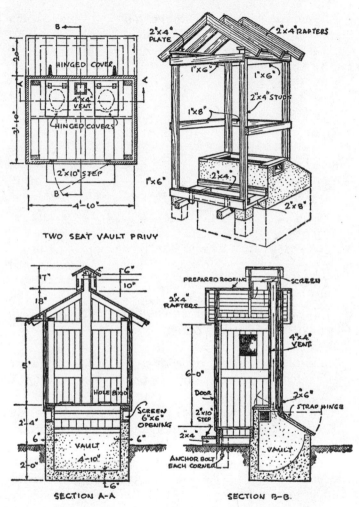

Construction details of a two-seat vault privy easily built near a cabin site

Material: All-heart Common redwood (No. 1 common with sap eliminated).

4 pieces 4 in. by 4 in. by 4 ft. (rough) for corner posts (3 ft., 11½ in. net).

10 pieces 2 in. by 10 in. by 7 ft. surfaced on 2 edges, for sides.

3 pieces 2 in. by 10 in. by 7 ft. (rough) for cover battens.

10 pieces 2 in. by 10 in. by 3 ft. surfaced on 2 edges, for ends.

32 pieces 2 in. by 6 in. by 3 ft. surfaced on 2 edges, for bottom and cover.

15 pieces 2 in. by 6 in. by 3 ft. surfaced 1 side for baffles.

42 linear ft. 1 in by 2 in., for baffle guides.

1 piece 1 in. by 6 in. with 6 ft. for 4 blocks at inlet and outlet.

Total board feet required, 374.

Tile: Two 4-in. vitrified salt-glazed single Y-branch sewer tile for inlet and outlet.

Quantity of 4-in. bell-neck sewer tile and 4-in. standard drain tile is dependent on position of tank with reference to source of sewage, and type and size of disposal field.

The liquid effluent from a septic tank, no matter what type, is discharged into a disposal or distributing field. This consists of a system of sewer pipe or drain tile laid with the joints open. It functions as a sewage filter for the sub-soil disposition of the waste matter. Proper construction is essential for success. The field should not be placed near a well or other source of drinking water.

A porous soil is best for a disposal field. The average

soil is not the ideal kind, so it is advisable to provide plenty of area, say 500 sq. ft. for each person served by the system. A good grass sod, with no trees or shrubbery, should be cultivated on the area after the tile sections are in. When the soil is of a dense, clay-like nature, it is plowed or otherwise loosened, and perhaps under-drained in a manner similar to that employed for cultivated fields.

After about 10 ft. of outlet tile are laid from the septic tank, a branched system of tile, resembling in form a pitchfork having two or more tines, is constructed. Assuming that the septic tank will discharge 20 gallons per person into the disposal field at one time, the branched system can consist of 50 ft. of 3-in. tile per person, the branches being laid 10 ft. apart. Second-quality sewer pipe in 2-ft. lengths, or good quality drain tile in 1-ft. lengths, is suggested by government authorities.

Proper construction of tile joints is important. When more than two branches are laid in the disposal system, a diverting box—a common distributing center for all branches—is employed. Tile from the tank to this box can be laid with cemented joints. Then, from the distribution point for a distance of a few feet along each branch, lay the tile with joints close, but do not cement them. Continue with joints spaced ⅛ in. apart, until the last 20 ft. is reached, when the joints are ¼ in. apart. Each branch can be ended in a T-section, one end of which projects above the ground to act as a ventilator, a cap of some sort keeping out dirt. An elbow can be used instead. This ventilator also acts as a marker for finding the tile line if it is necessary to dig it up. Each open joint must be protected from loose particles. This can be accomplished by covering the upper part with an 8-in. piece of tar paper that extends about ¾ the distance around the tile. Another method is to lay a board over the joint. A third method is to use bell-end sewer pipe and separate the joints a fraction of an inch, centering the nozzle end of each pipe in the bell of the other by putting a few pebbles at the lower part of the joint.

When the soil is sandy, a fall of 1 in. every 10 ft. is satisfactory. For dense soil, the fall is 1 in. every 60 ft., and the openings in the tile joints are increased slightly. For very poor drainage conditions, the tile can be laid in a bed of cinders, slag, gravel, crushed stone, or broken brick, in a ditch a foot wide at the bottom. Depth of the tile below the surface varies from 1¼ to 3½ ft., according to climate. Each branch of the disposal system should not be more than 100 ft. long.

Do not add disinfectants to the sewage that is to be treated in a septic tank. Such disinfectants may kill the beneficial bacteria on whose growth the action of the tank depends.

The U. S. Department of Agriculture suggests that builders of septic tanks or other disposal systems obtain sufficient information before they spend money on the project. Local county agricultural agents, health authorities, state agricultural colleges, the U. S. Public Health Service, and the Department of Agriculture are sources of reliable information on such subjects.

Cooking Aids

Kitchen stoves and other cooking and housekeeping aids need not be of an elaborate nature for average

cabin use. The type of stove will be determined by the
fuel to be employed. Wood, coal, gas, kerosene, gasoline, and electricity are possible sources of heat. Of
course, electricity and natural gas are more convenient,
but not always available. Neither is coal, in some sections.

One of the most promising and convenient types of
fuel for cabin or camp use is bottled gas. Within
recent years it has become familiar on farms, where a
regular service is maintained for replacing exhausted
steel bottles with charged ones whenever the necessity
arises. A pair of containers is mounted in a cabinet
outside the house, and connected to the gas stove,
water heater, etc. Only one bottle is permitted to discharge into the pipes at a time. When it is empty, the
other bottle is cut in, and the company supplying the
gas is notified, so that the empty bottle can be re-
placed.

Small bottles of acetylene or other fuel gas are obtainable at reasonable cost. A tank of acetylene 6 in.
in diameter and measuring 24 in. overall will cook a
surprising number of meals, when connected to a
suitable hot plate. One-burner hot plates can be
operated directly from a tank, but two- and three-
burner types require a reducing valve. An acetylene
tank can be used also to operate powerful lamps and
searchlights.

Hot water, usually considered a city luxury, can be
provided in the cabin at a cost surprisingly low. There
are available various kinds of heaters using wood, coal,
gas, or kerosene as a source of heat. A kerosene heater
suitable for operation in conjunction with a tank costs
less than $20.

There is one source of heat to which the average cabin or cottage owner never gives a thought. It is the sun. Since most of the vacationing will be done in summer, a simple solar heater will prove efficient in many localities, particularly the South. Such a heater consists simply of several lengths of black iron pipe connected by U-shaped couplings so that a grid arrangement results, placed where the sunlight will strike it a good part of the day. A 30-gallon hot-water tank placed above the level of the heating grid and not far from it, can be used as a storage place for the water. If well insulated with a jacket of asbestos or similar material, a tank will keep the water warm over night. Of course, there must be some way of circulating the water through the tank and heating element. In Florida, a single line of water pipe laid on the ground, in the sun, will deliver water hotter than the skin can bear.

Keeping food cool is a problem in the summer cottage. When a supply of ice is available, an ice box is the logical solution. Such a box can be built-in, with the main door opening into the kitchen and the ice compartment door opening on the porch. Anyone can construct a serviceable ice box by building a double-walled wooden case, with the space of 2 in. or more between walls filled with some insulating material such as rock wool. The box can have a hinged lid opening at the top, to cover the food compartment, and another lid for the separate ice chamber. The lids should be well insulated, but the partition between ice chamber and food compartment should not.

Other methods of keeping food cool include the digging of pits in the ground and the sinking of sealed

food containers or water-tight casings in the bed of a
stream. Perhaps a simple well can be dug in the yard,
and provided with an insect- and vermin-proof cover.
The well will work whether it is partly filled with water
or is a dry hole. Care should be taken to keep from
contaminating the food with impure well water or that
from a stream.

The above paragraphs may have demonstrated to
you that life in a cabin need not be the rough and sometimes dangerous existence that characterized the day
of your forefathers who originated the cabin idea as a
result of necessity. Modern science and industry have
made it possible for you to enjoy the major comforts
and safety of home even if you are in a wilderness
miles from nowhere, and at a cost that is not excessive.

CHAPTER XIV

BEAUTIFYING THE CABIN

MUCH has been said already about the beautifying of vacation homes—the use of colored drapes, proper interior wall finishes, and the like. For the benefit of the man who likes to do his own painting and to improve the looks of his cabin and surrounding grounds in other ways, more specific information will be included in this chapter.

The real log cabin or one covered with log siding can be left to weather without further treatment. The wood will, in time, take on a color and texture that probably will be some shade of gray or brown, depending of course on the type of wood. However, it is desirable at times to apply artificial coloring agents. These usually exert a preservative action as well.

Mention has been made of a mixture of one third turpentine and two thirds linseed oil as a filler that preserves wood and at the same time affects its color slightly. Pine and cedar, for instance, are darkened a bit by this filler, and as time passes the color becomes richer and darker. Be sure that the linseed oil and turpentine are of good quality. First of all, purchase the turpentine or oil from a reliable dealer, and insist on the best grade. Boiled linseed oil is thicker and richer in color than the raw oil, and usually is preferable. Prices for these materials vary constantly. Low-priced linseed oil is likely to be mostly cottonseed oil.

Shellac is another useful finishing material. Use it

as a filler beneath varnish and for sealing knots and resin streaks. It is excellent for waterproofing rustic furniture. One thing to remember about shellac is that it is not flexible, and therefore should not be used on anything that is subjected to bending. Painting authorities do not consider it suitable for the protective coating of floors for this reason. A durable and attractive finish can be given to furniture and woodwork by applying a coat of shellac, sanding lightly with fine sandpaper or steel wool to remove rough particles, and then applying two coats of good floor wax, polished between coats.

An inexpensive way of obtaining a supply of shellac is to purchase the dry shellac in flake form, and a quantity of denatured alcohol. Procure alcohol that was denatured specifically for shellac mixing and similar uses. Otherwise the denaturant may have so strong an odor that you will get the impression you are painting with something closely resembling over-ripe eggs. When you want to finish a chair or other article, place some of the dry shellac in a quantity of the alcohol and let it remain, with occasional stirring, until dissolved. You can produce any consistency you desire. It is much cheaper to purchase the ingredients separately than when they are combined and sold under a label.

Stain is a useful finishing material for the cabin and its equipment. With a few cents' worth of burnt umber, raw sienna, Van Dyke brown, and drop black, together with a quantity of turpentine and linseed oil, and maybe a few lake colors, you can make a wide variety of stains, and imitate almost any antique finish. The best way to determine what color and how much to use is to experiment. Mix some of the coloring material with turpentine, apply the resulting stain with a brush, let it soak into the wood for several minutes, and then remove the excess with a cloth.

Starting with the linseed-oil—turpentine mixture already mentioned as a filler for cabin exteriors, you

Your cabin can be provided with this simple and attractive gate and trellis

can produce various stains by using with it the oil pigments, lake colors, or dry colors. Burnt sienna gives a reddish brown. A darker brown is obtained by adding some black pigment. Black and red give other browns. To produce gray, add some white lead and black oil pigment or drop black to the turpentine or turpentine and oil. Small quantities of red are sometimes desirable to remove the cold tone of gray stain. Green is produced by mixing blue and yellow colors with turpentine, vary-- ing the relative amounts to produce different shades. Various green pigments such as chrome green can be used, and combined with black or yellow pigments to lighten or darken them.

Oil stains, which are essentially nothing but paints made very thin, are more convenient to use than water or acid stains because they can be applied with a brush and do not raise the grain of the wood. Various inter- esting effects can be worked out by using stains. For instance, the grain of white pine can be brought out by applying a stain consisting of pigments mixed with linseed oil, turpentine, and a little drier. Apply this to the wood evenly and let it remain until partly dry. Then rub with a cloth. The rubbing action forces the stain into the soft portions of the wood but removes it from the harder resinous parts, thus causing the grain to stand out more prominently. This is the action that takes place in almost all staining operations that involve wiping with a cloth.

An important outside use for stains is to color and preserve wood shingles. Creosote stains, procurable ready-mixed, generally are preferred because of their high preservative action. Shingles are stained by dip- ping and draining off excess stain, and are not soaked in the stain. They usually are dipped for two-thirds their length. Then they are piled loosely, so that air can circulate through them, and left to dry. After the shingles are laid, a second stain coat can be applied with a brush.

The cabin that is in a gloomy forest can be made more lively by introducing some color into the roof. Stain several batches of shingles different colors and apply them in random fashion, to produce a mottled effect. It will not be found out of harmony with the setting, if properly done, even when bright colors are used.

The use of paints for exterior and interior finishing is applicable to all types of cabins, lodges, and the like. Even a log house can be made more attractive and durable by proper use of paint on doors, window sash, and floors. The paint can be of the prepared type obtainable everywhere, or can be mixed on the job from white lead, linseed oil, color pigments, and drier. Turpentine is added with the oil for exterior prime coats, to hasten penetration. When using prepared paint, thin each gallon with 1 to 1½ quarts of turpentine, for the prime coat.

A highly important matter is to mix all paint thoroughly just before using. Paint, when left standing, settles, so that it should be mixed each time it is used. Proper mixing will eliminate a lot of painting grief.

Knots and streaks in pine and other woods, which are likely to ooze resin and cause later scaling of paint, should be treated with a coat of shellac or an application of turpentine before the paint is put on.

After the prime coat has dried for three or four days, putty all holes in the wood and apply the second coat. Use the paint as it normally is mixed, if but two coats are to be given. This gives a glossy surface. Addition of a little turpentine, say a pint to the gallon, will produce a slightly matte surface. If three coats are to be applied, the second coat can be thinned slightly with turpentine. When applying the paint, remember that the secret of producing a good job is not to pile it on thickly, but rather to brush it well into the wood. Paint in thick layers will peel sooner or later.

Floor paint differs from ordinary exterior paint in that it contains varnish that increases its durability. For shutters there is a special chrome-green shutter paint that is used for the finish coat.

There is a trick that can be used to make the small lake cottage or other summer home look larger. This

This rustic gate, somewhat elaborate in construction, will lend an air of distinction to your vacation home

trick is to use proper colors that give the impression of greater size. Cream, ivory, and other light, warm tints will do the trick, and will harmonize with a great many other colors. When there are no near-by trees, grayish greens and light grays can be used with a similar effect. A long, low, rambling effect, so desirable when the building nestles among the trees and has aspirations to be informal like an old-fashioned log cabin, can be enhanced by proper use of color. Thus a weatherboarded lake cottage can be divided by a horizontal line running around it about half-way between eaves and foundation, and the lower half painted a dark tone and the upper part a lighter color. Another way is to shingle the upper half and stain it a light gray and paint the lower half a darker tone. With these schemes a dark-colored roof should be employed. When the process is reversed and the lower part of the house made lighter than the upper half, a top-heavy effect is produced.

When the surface has been painted before, it is important that all old, scaly paint be removed by a vigorous work-out with a wire brush. The prime coat should be properly thinned with turpentine and thoroughly brushed into the wood.

Outside beautification of the cabin other than painting will consist mostly of the erection of fences and gates, arbors, pergolas for open-air dining, and the like; and the planting of shrubs and flowers.

For the woodland cabin, a yard that looks as nearly like the native woods as possible is desirable. When building the cabin do not cut or let anyone else cut any trees that are not dangerous or that do not stand where the cabin is to be placed. Likewise, refrain from trimming trees and removing branches near the ground, unless the branches constitute a hazard to heads of the cabin occupants. After the cabin is completed and has been in use for a while, you will be able to decide what trees should be removed or what branches cut away, so that you can enjoy a beautiful vista or take advantage of prevailing breezes. Native shrubs are desirable in the cabin yard. These can be transplanted without trouble. The same is true of wild flowers. Domesticated flowers such as pansies and begonias somehow look out of place in the woods. They may, however, appear perfectly at home by the lake cottage.

Trellises and rose arbors are useful for general decoration and for camouflaging outdoor privies and the walks that lead to them. The usual white-painted framework is out of place in a rustic setting. A better way is to use poles of some wood, such as California redwood, that does not require painting in order to keep it from rotting. Redwood and cypress are naturally resistant to weather and decay. Unpainted pine and other woods will last a long time, too. It is a good idea to apply hot creosote to the portions of poles and stakes that will be buried in the ground. Pergolas and summer houses can be built of poles or any of the various inexpensive woods. Such structures should, of course, always be in harmony with the main cabin, in design, material, and color.

CHAPTER XV

LONGER LIFE FOR YOUR CABIN

WHETHER you expect your cabin to bring you pleasure for a few years or a lifetime, it will pay you to take precautions against the natural enemies of wood structures, namely decay and insects.

Decay is caused by the growth in the wood of tiny plants called fungi. Moisture is absolutely necessary for such growth, and therefore only moist wood can decay or rot. This simple fact is overlooked by many cabin builders who, it would seem, deliberately arrange conditions that promote decay.

Numerous ways of retarding or preventing decay already have been mentioned. The use of suitable piers for supporting the structure off the ground is little more than common sense, yet we find many cabin builders laying the lower course of logs or the wall sills and joists directly on the ground. Of course, some woods such as cypress, redwood, and cedar will withstand such treatment for a long time; but this does not provide sufficient excuse for omitting a good foundation. For reasons that will become clear later, it is desirable to have the cabin at least 18 in. above the ground. The foundation should, of course, be of a type that will keep the sills dry. Also it should not be closed up tightly so that air cannot circulate beneath the floor. The lack of ventilation will enable the joists and other wood parts to remain constantly damp, and therefore invite decay.

Further guarantee against a constantly damp building is provided by proper drainage. Selection of the cabin site should be made with this in mind.

It is probably true that the majority of losses through decay in buildings, no matter what the type, could have been avoided by proper attention to con-

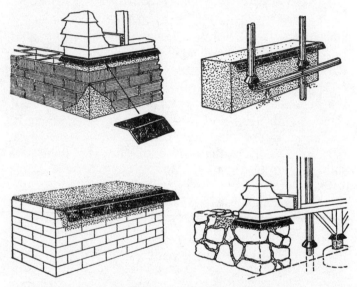

Illustrations show proper manner of construction to keep termites out of cabin and preserve its wood

struction details. Carelessly laid logs or improperly applied weatherboarding may create pockets that will hold water for long periods, and result in eventual rotting of the wood at such points. Log walls should be laid so that water will not remain in cracks and crevices for a long time. This means proper notching at corners, thorough chinking, and careful fitting at window and door openings. During a rainstorm, water may collect in many places, but if it dries out within a reasonable time, no harm will result. It is only the permanently damp places that invite the destructive fungi.

Window and door casings should be assembled and set in place with care. It will pay you to apply white lead to all joints, where there is likelihood of water entering and remaining. Fit weatherboarding and shingles tightly around windows and doors. See that the roof is perfectly water-tight. Insist upon porch floors that are laid with open joints or that have the tongue-and-groove joints coated with white lead thinned with good linseed oil. Shingle roofs generally are laid on boards that have spaces several inches wide between them, so that air can circulate about the shingles and keep them dry.

In short, keep out moisture and you will keep out troublesome and costly decay.

Do not depend too much on preservatives such as oils, creosote, and paint. These substances may retard the entrance of moisture and the flourishing of decay organisms, but they by no means are infallible in preventing them. There seems to be a general belief that paint effectively seals wood against the entrance of moisture. This is not true. For one thing, a board used as part of a building seldom is painted on all surfaces, so that moisture and decay can creep in behind the paint layer. Perhaps you have seen lumber that is rotting beneath a perfectly sound coat of paint.

In general, the life of a cabin, cottage, hunting or fishing lodge, or bungalow can be prolonged by routine care that is familiar to everyone. Prompt replacement of damaged and decayed timbers, keeping the roof in constant repair so that it does not leak, and periodic applications of good paint, will work wonders in this direction. Furthermore, a well-kept summer home will make any vacation more enjoyable.

If your cabin doesn't rot to pieces, something may come along and eat it. That is, if you do not take reasonable precautions to prevent such losses. Insects

The black dots in this log are holes bored
by the ambrosia beetle

attack certain types of wood buildings just as readily as they do peach trees or potato plants.

Log cabins, rustic woodwork, and wood that has not been thoroughly seasoned are most likely to be attacked by the bug army, although there are, in some parts of the United States, insects that will work damage to any building, if they can get to it.

Fortunately it is possible to repel the insect hordes by a properly-conducted campaign. A thorough study of the destruction of wood by certain six-legged pests has been made by the Bureau of Entomology and the

Forest Service, U. S. Department of Agriculture. In addition, the various state universities, agricultural experiment stations, and private corporations have devoted much time, effort, and money to the development of effective ways of waging the never-ending battle to save wood and things made of it.

More than one proud owner of a rustic summer home made of logs has had his joy turned to sorrow by finding that his home contained year-round guests that showed their gratitude by chewing the logs to pieces. It is to prevent such disappointment and financial loss that cabin owners have been demanding information on insect control.

Among the woods most commonly used for log cabins, rustic furniture, and fences are, according to the U. S. Department of Agriculture, hemlock, fir, tamarack, spruce, pine, cedar, juniper, hickory, birch, oak and poplar. Naturally some of these woods are less likely to be attacked by insects than others. But they all require protection of some kind or other in most instances.

Proper cutting of logs and poles will do much to prevent insect damage. The best months for cutting, when the bark is to be left on, are October and November. Logs should be stacked where they are not in contact with the ground, and in such a manner that air will circulate about them.

When the poles or logs are to be peeled, they can be cut at any time and treated at once, after peeling, with a mixture of one part creosote and three parts of kerosene. The creosote, when thus diluted, is not exceptionally strong-smelling, and stains the wood only slightly. Peeled logs should not be left lying on the ground, or they may be attacked by pinhole borers.

Some beetles, such as roundhead borers and powder-post insects, will attack logs no matter when they were

Piece of hickory with bark and a bit of wood removed to show tunnel cut by an adult powder-post beetle

cut. Chemical warfare must be resorted to. There are two chemicals suitable for use. One is the creosote already mentioned. The other is crude pyridine, a colorless liquid that produces almost no stain. Both of these substances possess strong odors, and should be handled in the open. Precautions should be taken to keep them off the skin and particularly out of the eyes. Either creosote or pyridine can be diluted with three parts of kerosene for treating wood.

Apply creosote or pyridine to the logs, poles, or timbers before they are installed in the building, and let them dry thoroughly in the open. The best way is dipping. Long, narrow troughs of sheet metal can be constructed and used as dipping vats. They should be just large enough to admit the pieces. When the wood is in position in the building, it can be treated by application with a brush or spray outfit, but such treatment is less effective than the dipping method before erection because all parts of the wood are not reached.

If the insect invasion has started, and the cabin owner finds that his walls are alive with beetles or their grubs, different tactics and ammunition have to be employed. Two more chemicals enter the scene. They are crude orthodichlorobenzene and paradichlorobenzene. The first is a colorless liquid that, like pyridine, should be kept off the skin and out of the eyes. It will kill grass and other vegetation if it comes in contact with it. Paradichlorobenzene is a white, crystalline substance with a strong odor. It is used in anti-moth preparations and for killing peach-tree borers. When employed for treating wood that has become infested with insects, it is dissolved in three parts by weight of kerosene. These two substances kill the insects by means of poisonous gas that they liberate slowly.

Orthodichlorobenzene or a solution of paradichlorobenzene in kerosene can be applied to the wood with a brush or spray gun. Thorough covering is essential. A gallon will cover about 50 sq. ft. of wood or log surface.

The remaining horde of insect pests that are likely to attack your cabin if it is in certain parts of the country, particularly the south, is composed of termites or "white ants." They look like ants, but are closely related to roaches. The particular type most likely to invade your property lives in moist ground at least part of the time. Termites of this species eat

Here is an adult powder-post beetle. This is the pest that bored into the tree shown in the preceding picture

wood (cellulose), and will convert any building into a meal if it happens to be handy.

Termite invasion is not always as serious as professional termite eradicators might lead you to believe. Cases are on record of ancient buildings that have been inhabited by termites for a half-century, and probably much longer, and still are sound. On the other hand, a heavy infestation of termites may cause extensive damage to the wooden parts of a building and the furniture and books in it.

The winged males and females that swarm from termite colonies in spring or fall are not the real cause of damage, although they may serve as a warning that the building from which they swarm is invaded. The wingless worker termites are the ones responsible for the destruction of wood by tunneling.

These "white ants," as they are generally called, avoid light as a small boy shuns a washrag. They go so far as to construct tunnels through which to travel in darkness. Furthermore, these termites must have moisture in order to live, and they generally obtain it by descending into the ground. These facts are important in their control.

The insects enter buildings in a variety of ways. They bore directly into wood that is resting on the ground. If it is on a foundation that is cracked, they will wall up some of the cracks to form light-tight passages. If the foundation is sound, they may construct tunnels of earth and wood pulp over its surface, until the wood above is reached. They even have been known to erect these tunnels without support until they projected up from the ground nearly a foot. Buildings with basements sometimes are invaded through openings in the basement floor or wall.

The type of building that is most resistant to termites is one having no wood in foundation, basements, or elsewhere near the ground. The cabin that rests on 18- or 24-in. piers and has a porch floor and steps supported by concrete or masonry, is reasonably safe.

Prevention of termite invasion consists in establishing a barrier between the ground and wooden parts of the building. Treatment after invasion includes breaking of their lines of communication between the building and the earth. It is absolutely necessary that the insects be able to travel back and forth between their earthen homes and their source of food, if they are to exist. When this is prevented by breaking the earthen communication tubes and establishing barriers, termites remaining in the building will die off quickly because of the lack of moisture. The only exception is when the wood is kept damp by a leaky water pipe or roof, or when a damp basement can be reached by the insects.

The presence of termites is indicated by the swarming of the winged insects, by presence of the com-

Two of the wood-destroying pests. Left, an adult bark beetle, and right, an ambrosia beetle

munication tubes on foundation walls and pipes, or by sagging of floors, caving in of walls or other evidence of damaged wood.

Among the recommendations for termite control made by government insect experts are the following:

All wood nearer the earth than 18 in. should be made termite-proof by treatment with coal-tar creosote under pressure. Such treatment can be given at properly equipped plants to be found in termite regions.

Steps should be of treated wood or should rest on concrete footings that extend at least 6 in. beyond the steps.

Portland cement mortar should be used in masonry

foundations, and all seams should be well filled. Termites can tunnel through poorly-made mortar joints.

The space under a building should be excavated until a clearance of 18 in. is produced, if that clearance does not exist already.

To prevent the building of shelter tubes by the termites, sheet-metal shields should be installed around the tops of foundation walls, around water pipes and wherever else a tube might be constructed. The shields consist of non-corroding sheet metal that is bent downward at a 45-degree angle, and that projects at least 2 in. in a horizontal direction from the surface being protected. Such shields can be installed on structures already built.

By proper selecting of wood you can avoid many of the troubles caused by decay and insects. Some woods naturally are resistant to these natural enemies, because of their chemical make-up. California redwood, southern cypress, and long-leaf pine are particularly resistant to termites. Redwood, cypress, cedar, and some other woods are likewise resistant to decay. The logical thing to do, when economically possible and when such woods can be employed in the type of cabin you have in mind, would be to use material that is resistant to both decay and insects. Of all the woods available, cypress, redwood, and some of the pines rank highest in this respect. When purchasing logs and poles for cabins, examine them to determine whether they are infested with borers.

Before you build your cabin, if it is to be in unfamiliar territory, make inquiries about the probability of termites and other pests. In this way you can learn much about the trouble and expense that will be required for adequate protection.

CHAPTER XVI

HUNTING AND FISHING LODGES

ESSENTIALLY the hunting or fishing lodge does not differ from any other cabin type. Therefore any of the plans and constructional details applying to the various cabins, week-end cottages, lakeside bungalows, and even tourist homes might be adopted for the lodge. In fact, it sometimes is difficult to draw a definite line of distinction between these various types of buildings.

A lodge is primarily intended to provide shelter and a place to sleep for the hunter or fisherman. It may be built by him for his personal use, on land leased or purchased, or it may be constructed by the land owner and rented to visiting fishermen and hunters. Such a lodge, which need cost little more than $150, might prove as profitable as a tourist cabin along a busy highway.

Because little more than shelter and bunk room is desired by the sportsman who spends most of his time in the woods, fields or along streams, the hunting lodge can be the essence of simplicity. For two to four men, a one-room structure with built-in or folding bunks, wardrobes or plenty of wall pegs, a table and a corner to prepare grub, will suffice.

For about $200, it is possible to build such a cabin, using log-cabin siding or similar material for covering the walls. A good width is 12 ft. and a suitable length

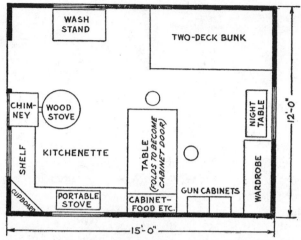

Floor plan of hunting lodge that would cost about $200

When completed, the $200-hunting lodge would look like this

is 15 ft. This will provide space for two bunks, one on each side of the room at one end. When four men are to be accommodated, the bunks can be double deckers;

or a single double-deck bunk can be used for two men, leaving floor space for other uses.

A window in the end wall, between the heads of the bunks, admits light and air. Beneath this window can be placed a table, chest of drawers, or any other convenient piece of furniture. At the foot of each bunk a wardrobe can be built, to act both as a clothes container and a kind of partition to separate the bunks from the remainder of the cabin. By each wardrobe is a window. On one side, beneath the window, is a wash stand, with perhaps a mirror hung near-by. A good place for a shaving mirror is on a wood support that stands out a few inches from the window, or which can be swung down in front of it. This permits both sides of the face to be lighted so shaving is easy.

On the other side of the cabin, opposite the washstand, is a miniature kitchenette consisting of a shelf or table, a portable stove of some kind, a cupboard for storage of food, perhaps a sink, and a can opener. In the center of the room, towards the front, can be placed a stove, its pipe entering a chimney supported on a platform built out from the end wall. Simple, light-weight chimneys can be supported on platforms in such cases; but they should be well insulated from all near-by wood. A table that folds against the wall or serves as the door of a cupboard is suitable for dining purposes. The doorway can be at any place in the front wall, provided it is not blocked by the stove or other equipment.

Because most hunters and fishermen travel to their cabins in automobiles, it is well to have a place to store the car. For such an arrangement, nothing could be more serviceable than one of the various tourist cabins

Here is an attractive tourist home that can be built at small cost

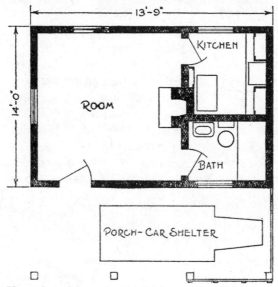

Floor plan of foregoing tourist home shows it is commodious and convenient (*Courtesy, California Redwood Association*)

described in another chapter. Such cabins frequently have car sheds or shelters built on one side as an integral part of the main structure. The cabin can, of course, be arranged inside in any convenient way. If the basic plan is a simple cabin rather than a tourist home, it should be an easy matter to build an extension roof at one side to form a car shelter.

The joy of a hunting or fishing expedition can be increased by giving some attention to built-in equipment and to proper sanitation. Everything that was said about the desirability of pure water and proper sewage disposal applies to the hunting lodge, although it would be uneconomical in most cases to install elaborate disposal or water supply systems.

Because the fisherman may catch a bass or trout occasionally, or the hunter bag a deer or duck, some effective means of disposing of waste materials resulting from the cleaning of such quarry should be available. Fish never should be cleaned on the bank of a stream because the decaying animal matter will increase pollution. Likewise no one wants the cabin yard to smell like a garbage dump. Perhaps the most effective way of disposing of fish and animal cleanings is to burn them. A simple incinerator can be built near the cabin, using field stones cemented with mortar or piled loosely and perhaps banked on three sides with earth. The incinerator should not be placed where wind may blow sparks on the cabin or other inflammable material. Before leaving on the day's expedition, the occupants should see that the fire is extinguished. Drowning it with water is the recommended method of making certain of this.

Here is another type of a simple tourist home that any one can build

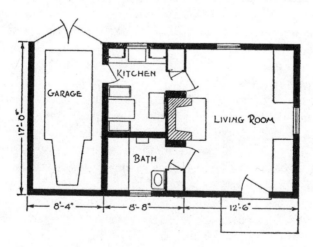

Floor plan of the above home, showing the one-car garage
(*Courtesy, California Redwood Association*)

Because hunting and fishing lodges are unoccupied for parts of each year, they should be equipped with strong doors and window shutters, to keep out intruders. It is not a bad idea to provide a cap for the chimney, a cast concrete slab will do, to foil the efforts of birds and small animals that might try to invade the lodge.

CHAPTER XVII

PROFIT-MAKING TOURIST HOMES

THE motorist of today demands more than a leaky tent under a tree for protection at night. On the other hand, he is reluctant to spend several dollars for hotel accommodations. Therefore the tourist cabin, which offers hotel accommodation at tent prices, has come into popularity along every well-traveled highway. Building a tourist cabin is much the same as building any other cabin or related structure.

The man who is a professional cabin builder will find the creation of tourist camps a highly profitable business. One who becomes a specialist in the construction of cabins, and the related bath houses, toilets, store buildings, service stations, and community kitchens, should have little trouble in acquiring some of this money. The farmer or other land owner whose property adjoins a busy highway will find a cabin camp a source of extra income during many months of the year. Two persons can take care of 24 cabins, a gasoline station, and a store. A small night camp might easily be a spare-time proposition, requiring attention only in the morning and evening.

The essential requirement of a site for a tourist cabin is that it be on a highway. A close second in the matter of requirements is the presence of trees. Good drainage is, of course, necessary. There must be a source of pure drinking water and a sanitary way of disposing of sewage and garbage—matters usually

Your tourist homes would be more attractive if you built and equipped this bath house

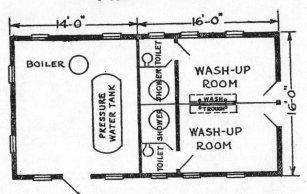

Floor plan of bath house that is extremely economical to build (*Courtesy, Long-Bell Lumber Co.*)

watched by the local health board. The presence of an attractive stream is a decided asset.

Many owners of tourist camps start with two or three cabins, and then add more as business improves. In this way their investment is kept at a low figure. A filling station, store and refreshment stand, centralized bath house, and a picnic grove will add to the profits.

Tourist cabins are not expensive structures. Being small, they can be built of short-length lumber that can be purchased more cheaply than standard lengths. The average tourist home is about 12 ft. wide and from 12 to 16 ft. long. Its windows are equipped with sash that can be opened, and fitted with screens to keep out insects. Likewise, there is a screen door. Windows and doors should be equipped with locks that can be operated without the aid of a kit of tools.

There is a growing demand among motorists for cabins that have an attached car shed. This can be open or enclosed, although most motorists probably would take the enclosed type if they had their choice. The shed frequently is a continuation of the roof, and in size is at least 8 ft. wide and as long as the cabin. An economical plan is to build twin cabins with a two-car shed between them, the car compartments being separated by a solid partition.

There are endless designs for tourist cabins. Commonly the framed-building construction is followed. Frames are built of 2- by 4-in. studs and rafters and 2- by 6-in. joists, covered with ordinary weatherboarding and roofed with composition shingles or roll materials. However, it is a good idea to avoid too conventional construction and attempt to produce something really distinctive.

For example, there is a "California type" of tourist cabin designed by Masten and Hurd for the California Redwood Association. It looks more like a comfortable week-end cottage or hunting lodge than a tourist home. The walls are of board-and-batten construction sup-

This cabin is designed for the use of two families. The wings are separated by a two-car garage (*Courtesy, Long-Bell Lumber Co.*)

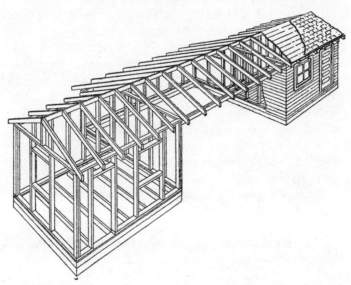

Detailed drawing showing the manner of building the two-family cabin

ported on a framework of 2 by 4's. Sills rest on red-wood-post footings, and the gable roof is covered with split shakes of the same material. The car shed is partly concealed by an attractive trellis on which a vine grows. Bandsawed verge boards, a well-balanced chimney, and shutters add to the attractiveness. The cabin contains a main room, a kitchenette, and a tiny bathroom. It measures 13 ft. 9 in. by 14 ft. at the sills, and the car shelter, which also can serve as a porch, is 8 ft. wide and extends the length of the cabin.

Painting is an important item of appearance. For the cabin just described, the following painting plan has been worked out: Roof shakes, left to weather naturally. Shutters and outside sash, stained green. Lattice of trellis, green. All other outside woodwork, whitewashed two coats. The interior is, for the most part, left in natural redwood. The floor is painted a dark green. Kitchen and bath are given three coats of cold water paint.

Whether the interior of a tourist cabin is ceiled or otherwise covered is a matter for the owner to decide. A ceiled job is usually preferable because considerable tourist traffic exists in early spring and late fall, when nights are chilly. Nothing will drive customers away more quickly than news that "the cabin was like an ice box." To further reduce the ice-box trend of a tourist cabin, apply building paper beneath the siding. Shingled sidewalls, because they are somewhat more efficient as heat insulators, will make a cabin cooler in hot weather and warmer in cold than most other types.

Builders and operators of tourist cabins generally do not recommend the use of plaster or any of the composition finishing materials for the interior walls. They say that wood is better because it will stand the knocks and bangs that the cabin is certain to receive from tourists. Incidentally, a cabin that is attractively finished is likely to receive better treatment than one that is not.

A sheltering garage for the car and room for two tourists are provided by this small cabin (*Courtesy, Long-Bell Lumber Co.*)

Cabins are built with either flat or gable roofs. Of the two, the flat one is the least desirable because it does not drain water rapidly and therefore may leak, and because it is hotter in summer. Also there may be some instances where a flat-roofed cabin would be damaged by heavy snowfall. The gable or hip roof is more expensive to build but less expensive to keep up. Also, the air imprisoned beneath it acts as a heat barrier and makes the cabin cooler. Any type of roof covering may be used, but it should be attractive. Wood shingles and shakes are popular.

The cabin stove probably will burn coal or wood, although in some localities natural gas is available. In either case a chimney is necessary. The recommendations made in the chapter on chimneys and fireplaces can be applied, with the exception that the chimney, being small, can be supported on a well-braced shelf extending out from the cabin wall. Precautions to prevent overheated wood should be taken. It is wise to follow suggestions made by a fire insurance company or other interested agency.

Next to a place to eat and sleep, the average motorist needs and desires a place to take a bath. There should be no need to state that bathing facilities should be sanitary. Whether each cabin has a bath or a centralized bath house is employed is a matter for the camp owner to decide. Centralized bath houses are seen frequently, probably because they are easier to care for and more economical to operate.

Such a bath house has been described by a lumber company that has made a study of the tourist-cabin situation. The house, as the floor plan indicates, consists of three compartments. One is the men's room and the second is for women. The third is the boiler room containing fuel bin, a pressure water tank and heater. In each of the wash rooms is a wash basin capable of accommodating several persons, and equipped with several faucets. At one end of the room is a toilet and next to it a shower compartment. The building is of conventional frame construction and is covered on the outside walls with 1- by 12-in. barn boards placed vertically. Shingles are used on the gable roof and composition roofing on the flat roof over the boiler room.

The gable construction could be extended to cover the boiler section, without much additional cost.

In addition to the types of tourist cabins already mentioned, the possibilities offered by real logs and log siding are limitless. A log-cabin tourist camp is more than a camp; it very often is a landmark. There is

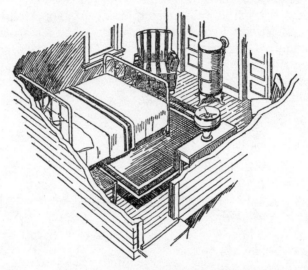

Interior view showing what your tourist home should contain if it is to prove attractive to your guests

something about a log building that causes the passing motorist to give it more than a casual glance, and to remember it thereafter. When there are two or three dozen such cabins, as would be the case of a fair-sized camp, the effect is the more marked and permanent. Of course, other things such as cleanliness, comfortable beds, and adequate bathing facilities must be provided.

But the mere appearance of a log structure is of great advertising value.

In addition to the cabins themselves, the well-equipped tourist camp includes a gasoline station, wayside lunch stand, store, and frequently a stand where near-by farmers can sell their produce. Some camps have built outdoor kitchens that proved popular. Such a kitchen need be little more than a roof supported by four posts, with a good-sized stove served by a masonry chimney. It may be desirable to build a wind break along one or more sides of the kitchen. It is good psychology to have the store and farm produce stand within convenient distance of the outdoor kitchen.

CHAPTER XVIII

WAYSIDE STANDS AND OTHER THINGS

AN INDUSTRY of astonishing proportions is strung out along the highways of the United States. This industry's purpose is to sell things and disseminate comfort and information to the passing motorist. Its visible plants include wayside lunch stands, gasoline stations, farm produce stands, signboards, comfort stations for tourists, ice houses, barbecue stands, dancing pavilions, ice-cream stands, popcorn booths, and salesrooms for flowers and shrubs.

Whether you build a wayside stand for yourself or for someone else who is willing to pay you for your efforts, you will find it worth while to apply many of the ideas contained in other chapters of this book. Of all the possible forms that a roadside stand may take, that involving the use of real logs or log siding is particularly desirable. Although some use has been made of such building materials along various highways, the field is virtually a brand-new one.

A gasoline station, lunch room or other sales center built of real logs is almost certain to stand out from every other similar place in the vicinity, and perhaps along the entire highway. There is something about a real log structure that commands attention and makes a lasting impression.

The development of log-cabin siding has opened an immense field to the builders of roadside stands. When properly used, such material is as distinctive as real logs, and in many localities is much cheaper.

Of course, wayside stands can be built of conventional material such as ordinary siding nailed over a wooden frame. Such places can be made extremely attractive and distinctive. However, the fact remains

This simple one-room cabin has all the essentials of the satisfactory and comfortable vacation home (*Courtesy, Shevlin Pine Sales Co.*)

that there are more ordinary frame shacks along our highways than attractive buildings of logs or some other material; and ordinary things seldom attract attention.

By making a few simple changes, many one-room cabins, designed primarily for recreational purposes, can be converted into practical wayside lunch stands. For instance, here is a 14- by 21½-ft. cabin designed

A combination lunchstand and lunch room that can be built at slight cost (*Courtesy, Northwestern Lumbermen's Association*)

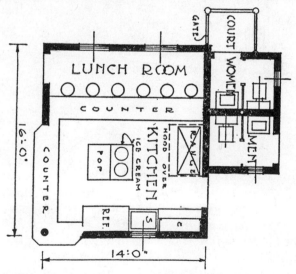

Floor plan of the lunch room shown in the preceding illustration

by Louis Boynton Bersback, Minneapolis, Minn., architect, for the Shevlin Pine Sales Company. You will note that there are two windows and a door in the front. To convert this cabin into a wayside lunch stand, all that is necessary is to take out the windows and build a counter that will project out from the wall.

This unusually attractive building is constructed of pine log siding. It is economical and easily built (*Courtesy, Shevlin Pine Sales Co.*)

Another way would be to build a porchlike arrangement in one of the front corners and erect a counter around it. This opening would extend about halfway across the front, so that the entrance door could be set in the remaining wall area. This door would lead to an inside lunch counter large enough to seat 6 or 8 customers. Serving both the inside and outside counters is a compact kitchen including a range, soda-fountain equipment, and other usual lunch-room devices. The cabin roof should be extended somewhat at the eaves so that it forms a shelter for the outside lunch counter.

A highly desirable part of any wayside stand is a section devoted to rest rooms for men and women. These can be made a part of the main structure, or

A pine log siding ice station that is a great convenience near a tourist camp (*Courtesy, Shevlin Pine Sales Co.*)

set at some distance from it. In either case, they should be properly designed from a sanitary standpoint. Log siding and similar materials are particularly adapted for such structures. Providing of rest-room facilities is more than an act of kindness towards motorists. It is sound business, for the traveler who makes a comfort stop is likely to purchase a few ice-cream cones or several full meals, depending on the time of day and the attractiveness of the stand

Even a sign board can be made attractive as is evidenced by the illustration above (*Courtesy, Red River Lumber Co.*)

A log-cabin gas station would be an excellent advertisement and at the same time fit into its environment (*Courtesy, Red River Lumber Co.*)

It is customary for farmers, whose land lies along a roadway, to erect stands at which to sell garden produce and other farm products. Competition in this field is keen, so the attractiveness of stands is of prime importance and value. A simple roadside produce market can consist of nothing more than a boxlike counter surmounted by a sheltering roof. Because the merchandise usually is removed from the stand at night, a permanently open structure can be used. Of course, if desirable, a small cabinlike building with a front opening surmounted by a hinged roof that can be swung down at night, can be employed. The shapes and sizes of roadside produce stands vary widely. Pleasing proportions are desirable, and freakish construction should be avoided. Often a plan for a full-sized cabin can be reduced by one third or one half, to produce an attractive stand. Log-cabin siding is particularly adaptable to such designs, although real logs, shakes, shingles, or ordinary weatherboarding can be employed as well.

One of the greatest advantages in using real logs or log siding is that these materials do not have to be painted or otherwise protected from the weather. This reduces upkeep costs. Such structures always look in good shape, even after years of exposure. By their very nature, they are supposed to be weatherbeaten.

Barbecue stands are constructed exactly like any cabin or other lunch stand, provision of course being made for the serving of sandwiches, refreshments, and full meals to customers. Such buildings generally are of fair size, and sometimes contain small dance floors. Log cabin construction methods are flexible enough to permit the erection of buildings of any size.

Gasoline stations present no problems to the person familiar with cabin building. A gasoline station often is of the same general design as a tourist cabin with attached car shed, so that the plans for tourist homes, given elsewhere in this book, may be adapted by increasing the dimensions somewhat.

Farmers who wish to sell their produce to tourists could do no
better than erect a sales cabin like this

Log-cabin sites are fittingly advertised by a
log-cabin sign like this set up at the side of
the road

The owner of a chain of lunch stands, filling stations,
or other commercial enterprise will find it profitable
to standardize on one distinctive type of construction.

He might operate the "Log Cabin Wayside Stores," or a series of "Shingled Shanties" for the dispensing of soft drinks. Once a motorist becomes familiar with one of the units of such a chain, he will recognize others instantly, and immediately feel that he is meeting an old friend.

An architect who was called upon to produce plans for an inexpensive yet attractive town hall specified pine-log siding set vertically and painted white, to produce a modernistic appearance. The job, when completed, lived up to all expectations, indicating that building materials primarily intended for rustic projects can be turned to modern purposes.

This scheme could be adapted to the wayside stand with gratifying results, provided the design was well worked out. For the small structure, narrow, round-log siding probably would be most suitable. Simply by varying the fundamental design and finish, a structure resembling a pole house or a modernistic building can be produced.

If you are in the business of erecting cabins for others, it may pay you to investigate the possibilities of roadside stands and their close relatives. A drive along any highway will reveal dozens of such places. Many of them, you will find, are sadly in need of overhauling or complete replacement. By talking the matter over with the owners, you may be able to bring home to them the wisdom of operating a stand that really is attractive and distinctive. By making a special study of the requirements of highway business places, you ought to have no trouble in establishing yourself in a well paying business. When you have finished erecting such a stand, attach to it some form of in-

offensive label or name plate that will tell others who
did the work. Then, when a man who has an idea
that he might find profit in operating a similar place
happens along, he will have little trouble in finding
someone to do the work for him.

CHAPTER XIX

"INSIDE" CABINS

THE log-cabin idea has been introduced into city houses and similar residences and commercial buildings because the rustic atmosphere pleases everyone. Basement recreation rooms, dens, and even whole houses, when finished with log siding or even real logs or slabs, have a charm never to be forgotten by the guest or disliked by the owner. The boy who has a log-cabin room in which to play and study will be the envy of all his playmates. With log siding and similar materials, it is possible to remodel any type of room tastefully and without great expense.

For a genuine rustic effect, slabs, which are sections sawed from logs when they are being reduced to square timbers, can be purchased at sawmills and lumber yards. These slabs are covered with bark on their curved surfaces. Care should be taken to see that they are not infested with insects. The slabs can be hewed or ripped with a saw to make them of fairly uniform width, with straight edges. The use of real logs generally is not economical or desirable when an interior is being refinished. However, if the rustic room is being established when the building is in process of construction, real logs can be worked in without much difficulty. The logs should, of course, be sound and free from insects. No particular precautions will have to be taken to prevent decay because they will be dry at all times. The third possibility is log siding in one of its various forms. Particularly pleasing is siding made of pecky incense cedar. In addition to being durable and attractive, the wood gives off a pleasant odor.

There are various ways of applying the siding or slabs, or laying the logs, so that a genuine-looking interior results. Logs should be staggered so that their ends come together in the natural way. They can be notched in the usual manner and arranged without projecting ends, if desired. Standard chinking methods can be followed. When genuine logs are used, adequate supports should be provided to carry their weight.

Log siding or slabs generally are laid in horizontal rows with their ends coming together evenly, where they are mitered to fit snugly. A better but somewhat more laborious way is to stagger the rows so that a more realistic effect is produced. The boards can be fitted together at the corners with the aid of a keyhole or scroll saw. Any carpenter who has had experience with fitting moulding can do the work.

Another way of using logs, slabs, or siding is to arrange the pieces vertically, like the elements of a pole house. Generally, however, this construction is not as pleasing as that more nearly approaching the conventional cabin form.

When space is available, a beamed ceiling is a decided asset. A gabled construction can be used, the cross beams being of genuine logs either peeled or with the bark left on; or the beams can rest against a horizontal ceiling surface of an appropriate texture and color. By placing the beams against a knotty-pine ceiling covering, the desired rustic effect will be produced. Instead of logs, beams can be made of hewn cypress, redwood, or pine, either left natural or stained to simulate weathered wood. A silver-gray stain or one of the lighter shades of brown will do.

To complete the cabin effect, a massive stone fireplace is almost an essential. Follow recommended

The illustration above shows how an interior may be made attractive by the use of log siding

methods when building this, and design it so that real wood fires can be enjoyed. There may be local building regulations that govern such work. Native stone set in cement mortar is about the only true log-cabin fireplace construction, although some rustic southern slave houses had rough brick fireplaces that were white-washed. It is safest to stick to stone.

The arrangement of rustic chairs, benches, and other furniture; lighting fixtures made from wagon wheels and the like, and the installation of mounted deer heads, mounted fish, guns, snowshoes, and other articles that add to the cabin atmosphere, are matters not difficult to carry out.

There is another use for log-cabin siding, namely the producing of modernistic interiors. The round-log siding usually is employed. It is set vertically, in most cases, and combined with modernistic furniture and fittings. White, black, and colored enamels, and aluminum paints are used as finishes. The combining of curves with straight lines is effectively carried out, as demanded by the modern school of decoration. By using log siding, a modernistic interior can be produced at a reasonable cost. The job should not be attempted, however, without previous study of modern decorative art, for it is easy to produce a monstrosity instead of a charming room.

CHAPTER XX

SUMMER HOMES IN NATIONAL FORESTS

WHERE to build is often the biggest problem that the prospective cabin owner has to solve. The answer is easily found if there is a national forest within reach.

A national forest is a government-owned region of natural scenic beauty, set aside so that its wonders may be enjoyed by everyone. The government harvests forage and timber from these forests. Wild-life refuges abound in them. In fact, they are the last sanctuaries of much of the game and other wild life of the United States. In some of the forests are fish hatcheries.

Anyone can get permission to erect a summer home on government land within national forests. These summer homes generally are of the log-cabin type. They must be rustic in nature, so as to blend with the surroundings.

Suppose, for example, that you are traveling through one of the national forests, and have come upon an area set aside by the United States Forest Service for the erection of summer homes. You like the looks of the place, and decide that you want to build a summer cabin there. Inquiry reveals that you must get a summer-home permit.

This is written permission for you to build a cabin on government property set aside for the purpose. You cannot buy the land, but you can lease it for cabin-building purposes. These special-use permits are granted for an indefinite period, or for a definite term. Usually the indefinite permit is satisfactory. Summer-home permits run for 5 to 15 years with privilege of renewal. Rentals for summer-home sites run from $5 to $25 per year, with the average about $15. Payments are due the first of each year.

Having selected a place where you would like to build a cabin, you can make application for the necessary permit, to a forest ranger or any forest officer. The best plan is to apply to the proper forest supervisor, addressing your request to the supervisor's headquarters; or you can obtain general information about forest-home sites from the Regional Forester, at the address given later in this chapter. Application blanks are not necessary for making summer-home site applications.

The regulations you will have to obey in connection with your cabin project are not stringent. They are imposed merely for the purpose of assuring safety and enjoyment to all who use the forest as a recreation place. There is some control over the type of cabin you may build. This is for the purpose of preventing shanties and gaudy structures that would be entirely out of keeping with the spirit of the forest.

For this reason, your building plans must be approved by the Forest Service before you may go ahead with the construction. Such things as appearance, fire menace, and sanitation are considered. The buildings themselves must be substantial, with well-designed doors, windows, floors, roofs, masonry, or brick chimneys. Fly-proof toilets and sanitary garbage containers must be provided. Strict rules are enforced in connection with location of toilets and water sources. No toilet is allowed closer than 100 ft. to a well or spring.

Gaudy colors are not permitted on cabins when they are in a position where they can be seen by forest visitors. This is in keeping with the general idea of presenting a true woodland scene to the visitor. Likewise, there are regulations concerning the erection of signs, house numerals, and the like. Rustic numerals and name plates are preferable. Commercial signs cannot be put up without special authorization. Keeping farm stock, such as chickens and cattle, is authorized only by special permit.

Forestry officials, in carrying out their plans for preserving the rustic scene, favor cabins of real logs, when such material is available; board-and-batten cabins when soundly constructed; shingle-covered frame cabins, and those using log-cabin siding. In short, any cabin that is well-built and reasonably conservative in design and color scheme will be acceptable.

When log-cabin material is available in sufficient abundance, permit owners may get authorization from the Forest Service to cut trees. Nominal charge is made for such standing timber. However, it has been the experience of forest officials that the genuine log cabin usually is more costly than frame types except in regions where sawn lumber is not available. The tree may be available for a very low price, but the cost of cutting it and transporting it to the cabin site will be considerable in most cases.

Permission is granted to cut trees on the cabin site only when the trees are distinct menaces to life and property, obstruct vistas, or interfere with desirable breezes. Small trees are not to be stripped of their limbs near the ground, but only should be cleared of dead branches. The general landscaping of the cabin lot should be carried out with the idea of producing a natural appearance. Forestry officials encourage the growing of shrubs or bushes that serve as screens to separate the cabin from others and from roads and streams. Frequently these screen-forming plants can be transplanted from other parts of the lot. Regulation is exercised over appearance of fences, particularly when the cabin is near a well-traveled trail or road. Barbed-wire fences are not permitted.

In order to see that the regulations are obeyed, that the cabin and site are kept in an attractive and sanitary condition, forestry officials pay inspection visits at least once every year. Continued failure to live up to the regulations will result in cancellation of the summer-home permit.

Although the land remains the property of Uncle Sam, the cabin belongs to the permit holder who built it. In some states, taxes are levied upon cabins, but not upon the land. The holder of a special-use permit merely pays the required fee each year, in order to renew his permit. Term permits are renewable as long as regulations are not violated. The permit holder may obtain government sanction to transfer his permit to another person to whom he has sold the cabin and other improvements. The permit holder must present a letter or bill of sale to the forest supervisor before such transfer can be completed.

In addition to the national forests, there are various state forests in which cabin sites are available. Inquiry should be made at the state department of agriculture or similar governing body.

In some of the Eastern national forests, summer-home sites are not as plentiful as in those farther west as the forests are smaller in area and the number of visitors from large centers of population is greater. The trend in these districts is rather towards the establishing of recreational facilities that will serve a large number of people equally. Therefore, lodges, public camp grounds, and hotels, provided for the benefit of visitors and vacationists, are much in evidence. However, numerous choice summer-home sites are made available in Eastern forests, when they will not interfere with the privileges of the majority. The large number of relatively small forest preserves extending for practically the entire length of the Appalachian Mountains offer wonderful opportunities to the inhabitants of crowded cities of the South and East. Only in the White Mountain Forest in Maine and New Hampshire and the Wichita Forest in Oklahoma are summer-home sites entirely lacking. For every other national forest, permits are issued.

National Forests of the United States are divided into regions. The Regional Forester in charge of each division is prepared to furnish detailed information concerning summer-home permits, and the authorization to establish hotels, resorts, or other commercial enterprises on government land. National Forest Regions, the states in which forest preserves in the respective regions are located, and the addresses of regional foresters are as follows:

Region 1—Northern Region, including forests in Idaho, Montana, South Dakota, and Washington.

Regional Forester, Federal Bldg., Missoula, Montana.

Region 2—Rocky Mountain Region, including forests in Colorado, Nebraska, Oklahoma, Wyoming and South Dakota. Regional Forester, Federal Bldg., Denver, Colorado.

Region 3—Southwestern Region, including forests in New Mexico and Arizona. Regional Forester, Gas and Electric Bldg., Albuquerque, New Mexico.

Region 4—Intermountain Region, including forests in Arizona, Colorado, Idaho, Utah, Wyoming and Nevada. Regional Forester, Forest Service Bldg., Ogden, Utah.

Region 5—California Region, including forests in California and Nevada. Regional Forester, Ferry Bldg., San Francisco, California.

Region 6—North Pacific Region, including forests in Washington and Oregon. Regional Forester, Post Office Bldg., Portland, Oregon.

Region 7—Eastern Region, including forests in Alabama, Arkansas, Florida, Georgia, Louisiana, Pennsylvania, Maine, South Carolina, North Carolina, New Hampshire, Tennessee, Virginia, West Virginia, and Porto Rico. Regional Forester, Atlantic Bldg., Washington, D. C.

Region 8—Alaska Region. Forests in Alaska. Regional Forester, Goldstein Bldg., Juneau, Alaska.

Region 9—Lake States Region, including forests in Michigan, Minnesota, and Illinois. Regional Forester, Customs Service Bldg., Milwaukee, Wisconsin.

Whether or not you go into a National Forest with the intention of building a cabin, there are certain things that you should do in order to save trouble for yourself and others, and prevent forest fires.

The Forest Service, in making suggestions for the camper, sportsman, or tourist entering a forest, points out that his equipment should include a shovel, bucket, and an ax; that a camp-fire permit should be obtained; that all fires must be put out with water before being left unwatched; that he should assist forest rangers in reporting and suppressing fires; that camp grounds must be left in a clean and sanitary condition; that state hunting and fishing laws shall be observed, and that the smoker's code should be followed. There is a regulation against picking wild flowers or disturbing other growing things near highways or recreation spots. Efforts are made to preserve wild flowers and growing plants within 100 yards of roads, so that travelers may be able to enjoy them.

These suggestions and regulations will, if followed, make life easier for any vacationist, no matter where his cabin is located, or whether he has one at all.

CHAPTER XXI

SPECIFICATIONS AND ESTIMATES

IF YOU undertake to build a cabin or one of its relatives for someone else, it will be necessary for you to prepare specifications and an estimate of the cost of materials and labor. If you are building for yourself, it will pay you to work out carefully such a plan of action. Specifications and estimates are outlines that serve as a basis upon which to act. The one shows what materials will go into the building and explains how they will be used. The other lists the amounts and costs of these materials and of labor and other items of expense. Specifications tell the prospective builder just what he will get, and the estimate will show him approximately how much it will cost.

There is no building expert living who can estimate exactly how much a building will cost. There are so many variable factors that some guesswork will be involved. However, the estimator who has had considerable experience will be able to come reasonably near the truth. Large contracting companies employ experts who do nothing but figure probable costs. The individual who would do work for another must be his own estimator, basing his figures on current prices for labor and materials, and on his ability to anticipate results. At best, estimating is speculative in nature; but it is far better then haphazard guessing.

A contract between an owner and a builder is merely a legal instrument that binds the owner to pay so much for a certain piece of work such as the erection of a tourist home. Specifications are fundamentally a part of the contract, but they are more in the nature of a working outline for the contractor. They point out what he must do and how he must do it. Specifications such as the cabin builder will be preparing, either for his own use or as part of a contract, need cover only the fundamental points such as the type of cement mortar to use for fireplaces, and not go into exhaustive detail about things which are generally taken for granted.

Before making an estimate of the cost of a building project, the estimator should visit the site on which the building is to be erected. A study of this will tell him much about the probable cost of digging holes for foundation piers, hauling material to the job, etc.

Some other general suggestions for estimate-makers might include the following: Take the probable weather into consideration. The time of year will influence costs of excavating, hauling materials, etc. If men are hired for doing masonry, carpentry, or other work, they should be covered by insurance against accidents. Remember that a small job, like building a cabin, cannot be estimated as closely as a larger one where mistakes will tend to neutralize one another to some extent. In estimating the amount of sheathing required for a building, calculate all areas as if they were solid, deduct for openings, and then add about 16 per cent for floors, 22 per cent for roofs and 18 per cent for sidewalls. The same plan can be followed for shiplap siding. For flooring, add from 25 to 33 per cent to the actual area to be covered.

Suppose, for example, that you are going to build

a Colonial type tourist home. You might prepare specifications and an estimate like the following. Of course you would find, when carrying out the actual work, that numerous changes could be made with advantage, and that you guessed wrong on many of the items; but you would have a useful guide to follow.

Your first task is to prepare plans showing the front, rear, and end elevations of the building; the floor arrangement and details of special constructional features.

Then work out the specifications. The following example is necessarily not exhaustive in nature.

Specifications for Colonial type tourist cabin:

General: Dimensions shown by plans and figures are to be followed. If there is a disagreement, the plans will be accepted as accurate.

All workmanship is to be of highest quality, and materials are to be the best available.

The owner may make alterations or changes during the progress of the work, the cost of such to be added to or subtracted from the price as required.

Foundation: The cabin will rest on concrete piers set into the ground and provided with footings extending below the frost line. Footings not less than 18 in. square, extending within 6 in. of the ground surface, and made of concrete composed of 1 part (by volume) Portland cement, 2 parts clean, sharp sand and 4 parts washed gravel. Piers not less than 1 ft. square and extending to height designated by owner. Pier concrete of same composition as footing, and reinforced with 4 vertical steel rods ½ in. in diameter, placed 2 in. from respective corners and tied together with heavy wire at 12-in. intervals.

Excavation: In addition to holes for piers, soil will be removed when necessary so that there is a clearance of at least 6 in. beneath all parts of building.

Fireplace Foundation: The fireplace will be supported on a footing of concrete 6 in. thick and 1 ft. larger each way than the hearth. Place footing below frost line. Concrete composition same as for piers.

Fireplace and Chimney: Use good quality common brick set in cement mortar composed in proportion of one 94-lb. bag Portland cement, 9 lbs. dry hydrated lime, and 3 times their combined volume of clean, sharp sand. Flue to be lined with cylindrical fireclay lining having a cross-sectional area equal to $\frac{1}{10}$ area of fireplace opening. Chimney capped by brick set on edge in mortar. Fireplace lined on sides and back with firebrick. Hearth covered with cement mortar.

Lumber: All lumber, except where noted, is California redwood, well-seasoned. Sizes include:

Sills, 3 by 6, heart common.

Tops of sills, 2 by 4, heart common.

Floor joists, 2 by 6, heart common.

Plates and bridging, house and garage, 2 by 4, heart common.

Studs, 2 by 4, heart common. 18″ centers in house, 2′0″ centers in garage.

Rafters, 2 by 4, heart common, 2′0″ centers.

All other timbers not mentioned, to be furnished in standard size and good grade.

Outside walls: The walls are of board-and-batten construction. The boards, set vertically, are 1 by 12 select or clear redwood, set with rough side out. Battens are $\frac{1}{2}$ by $2\frac{1}{2}$ redwood, select or clear, nailed over joints in such a manner that weather cannot enter.

Roof: Roof is covered with 1 by 4 sheathing, heart common redwood, 8" on center. Redwood shingles, laid 4½" to weather, and nailed with copper or zinc-coated nails, 4 penny shingle-nail size. Valleys and chimney to be flashed with 16-oz. sheet copper, lapped and soldered, with rosin flux, at joints. 4 by 4 redwood gutter extends along eaves.

Windows: D. H. window frames, 3'6" by 5'1", with 6-light sash, glazed, and with weights and cords. Frames shall be of standard design. Front window is to be equipped with 1 pair of stock shutters, 1'6" by 5'1".

Doors: Door jambs to be 2'6" by 6'8" by 5⅜". Casings, both sides, to be 1" by 5". Entrance doorway hung with 6-panel stock door 1¾" thick, with leaded glass transom. Inside doors are 1-panel, 1⅜" stock.

Entrance: In front of the main doorway is a landing of common brick, laid flat in cement mortar mixed as already specified. Flanking the entrance are two lattice frames made of 2 by 2 vertical members and 1 by 1½ cross members, select or clear redwood.

Flooring: The floor throughout will be of 1 by 4 or 1 by 6 tongue-and-groove redwood, securely nailed with one 6-penny flooring brad at each bearing point. Flooring ends to be butted tightly against sidewall boards, and joint at angle sealed with ½-in. quarter-round moulding.

Inside Finishing and Fittings: Inside wall and ceiling surfaces to be covered with 1 by 12 redwood boards with moulded joints cut as shown in detail B. All door openings to be trimmed with plain 1 by 5 casings. Window casings to match door casings. Build medicine cabinet 1′2″ by 1′8″—6″ deep, with mirror in door; spice cabinet 1′10″ by 3′0″—4″ deep, single panel door; two kitchen cabinets 2′0″ by 3′6″—12″ deep, single panel doors. Install stock drainboard 1′10″ by 2′6″ by 1 ¹⁄₁₆″, sugar pine. Run 1 by 4 moulding cut to detail A, around room in angle between sidewalls and ceiling. All interior finish to be best grade clear redwood, kiln-dried and finished smooth. Leave living room walls and ceiling natural redwood finish. Apply two coats white paint to bath and kitchen walls. Finish all floors two coats floor paint, dark olive green. Nail holes in painted surfaces to be puttied after prime coat is applied.

Outside Finish: Apply 2 coats dark green stain to roof, lattice and shutters. Board and battens, door and sash, two coats white lead and oil.

The foregoing specifications could, of course, be expanded to include greater detail. Only some of the essential items have been listed, others being omitted because of space restrictions. Additional divisions that would enable everyone concerned to get a clearer picture of the proposed building might include cellar excavation and floor construction (in buildings where a cellar is used); details of automobile shed corner posts and other parts; cornice construction; screens and blinds for windows; plumbing, including water supply and sewage disposal facilities; heating equipment, etc.

From the specifications, plans, materials list, local labor conditions, nature of the site, and other conditions influencing costs, the builder next prepares an estimate. This estimate is his personal calculation of the probable cost of the tourist home. He bases it upon all the data available, and does not begin its preparation until all facts are at hand. To the computed cost he adds a percentage for profit and for unexpected expenses. The profit will vary, and can be anywhere from 10% to 20% or more of the actual cost of labor and materials. An estimate at best is only an approximation.

INDEX

INDEX